My Journey to the Promised Land

To Anthony
Enjoy "My Journey"
and may yours be blessed.
Dorothy Schuler
3/14/2016

My Journey to the Promised Land

A Story of Faith, Family and Love

By

Dorothy Schuler

ISBN 978-1456527273

Library of Congress Control Number
2011903262

Printed in the United States of America

Purchase book online at:
http://dorothyschuler.net
or
www.Amazon.com

To my mother, Dena Meinhardt, who brightened my childhood with her true life stories.

Contents

Preface

"Here I am Lord! Is it I Lord?

I have heard You calling in the night.

I will go Lord, if You lead me.*

The song, taken from Scripture, has become one of my favorite hymns, often playing uninvited in my mind, and there are other melodies I cannot turn off even though the words have long ago escaped me. A little like the memories of my life, the tune plays on.

I am Dorothy Catherine Meinhardt Schuler, now in my 96th year, mother to over 100 living family members, married to C. John Schuler almost 50 years, until he passed away 25 years ago on May 9, 1986. He left me with our beautiful family of twelve children, their spouses, and over two dozen grandchildren.

I began in my eighty third year to recall and record the vivid memories of my childhood and the stories about our ancestors that I heard growing up. My mother was a wonderful storyteller and could fascinate us with tales of the "Old Country" which she left to cross the Atlantic Ocean at the age of six. She told us about her arrival in Kansas and growing up in the days of long skirts and high button shoes and how she rode the horse side-saddle. With these accounts in mind my first intention in writing was to share with my progeny the

---

* Lyrics (a reference to Isaiah 6:8) and music are by Daniel L. Schutte, copyright 1981.

history of our forebears. I marveled that during my lifetime I had touched seven generations of family—from my great grandmother born in 1828 in Germany to the youngest of my offspring born in Seattle in 2008—and I wanted to strengthen the connection among the generations. As I wrote I gained increasing respect and admiration for the courageous ancestors who possessed the vision and the audacity needed to pull up stakes, leave home and everything familiar in order to build new lives and find community in a far off place across the sea, their own "promised land." Their journeys, marked by faith and love and guts, inspired me and gave me strength to reflect on my own life.

For mine, too, has been a journey in search of a promised land; a search for a place to raise my family in material security and in a community of shared values and faith; a search for the path to spiritual understanding and communion with God. Of course, journeys are never straight-forward without bumps along the way. Count on it, there will be detours, hills, valleys and forks in the road. Thus has it been in my life. Many circumstances and decisions determined the path that has led me to the present moment—some unexpected or undesired, others welcomed and cherished. Who would have thought that a sickly child would live to have twelve children—and do it the old fashioned way to boot, one at a time? How would I have known that my struggles growing up in the Kansas dust bowl during the Depression would be transformed into constant gratitude for the breathtaking beauty of life in the Pacific Northwest? How could I ever have foreseen that I'd be able to find and live in a wonderful home that would serve as a welcoming anchor for the family for more than six decades? How could I ever have imagined that I'd find a community of friends bonded together in work and laughter and tears and faith within our parish at St Benedict's?

Throughout life, I have noticed that the journey is always in progress and even when we set our heart on a destination, it is never fixed. Just when we think we've arrived at the promised land, there is another one to be reached right around the corner. Often, we don't even know where we are going. When my great grandfather acquired his first homestead after traveling so far from the land of his birth, surely he thought it was his dream fulfilled and the end of his journey; yet he was called to leave that place and move once again—and then again—until he found his ultimate fulfillment farming the fertile fields of Kansas and working to build the community of Sacred Heart Parish in the little town of Newbury. As a young mother it was not part of my dream to still be bearing children into my late forties, fearing that I might not live to raise them to adulthood. Instead, I lived to see not only my own children, but my grandchildren and even great grandchildren grow up, become adults and thrive. To this day, the fulfillment that comes from family, including the children for whom I provided day care over the years, has been one of my greatest blessings.

The lesson of my life is to trust in the guidance of the Lord, who knows better than we do what it is we need and where we need to end up. For me, the words of the song continue to ring loud and clear and I pray I will always be able to respond in kind. It is in that spirit that I share tales of my journey.

I will go, Lord, if you lead me.

CHAPTER ONE

NEWBURY AND PAXICO

Roots

My Grandfather August Meinhardt must have liked what he saw when he arrived in the 1870s in that Kansas county with its vast valleys and wooded hills. It was a region of table-flat land with fields weaving geometric patterns of radiant yellow as wheat swayed under the golden sun, of beautiful valleys surrounded by rolling hills and green pasture land. Creeks edged with borders of timber made their way to the rivers. Subject to flooding after a sudden downpour, they would quickly drain into the bigger streams or flow out of their banks to soak the fields.

I can only imagine his excitement when he saw the land that would become his. It was mostly level, surrounded by gently rolling hills to the north and east. In the western view, earth met the sky as the sun descended behind the open fields. The southern border was a range of steeper heavily wooded hills rising above Mill Creek. They hid from view the range lands, the tall grass prairie that showed evidence of the buffalo which had recently roamed those thousands of acres that lay beyond.

Mill Creek held a great fascination for me as a child. It was usually swift enough to hear its song before it came into view. Beginning with just a murmur, the sound of the flowing water mingling with the birds' songs gave to me a feeling of great delight. The reflection of trees in the wider pools painted a picture for me, not on canvas, but forever in memory. The border timber was a sanctuary for a variety of song birds—cardinals, wrens, skylarks, doves and others I cannot name. Downstream, it was always a thrill to go over the stone arch bridge and view the big waterwheel and old mill, an ancient stone building with its weathered, moss-covered roof. Little did I understand the function of the water wheel, nor that it was connected to the building. It was enough just to watch it turning, spilling water forward while it continued to rotate in the flow of the creek. Mill Creek, which appeared to be a river itself, eventually emptied into the Kansas River 15 or 20 miles downstream.

Early German settlers selected Newbury as the site of their future town. The area, formerly a Pottawatomie Indian Reservation, had been off limits to settlers until 1869 when the U.S. Government allowed the Indians to sell their land. With the hope of establishing a Catholic community in the area, the Jesuit Fathers spread word to potential immigrants about this opportunity to purchase land. As a result, a number of families from various parts of Germany found their way to Middle America and to Newbury Township in Wabaunsee County to settle, build homes and cultivate the land.

My grandfather, August Meinhardt, was one of these early settlers. He was born in Silberhausen in the Eichsfeld region of Germany on May 29, 1853 and came to America at the age of 18. I think he was a courageous young man with hope for a better life when he left parents, four brothers and a sister knowing that he would never see them again. There is no record that any of them ever got to America so their "Auf Wiedersehen" was truly "till we meet again"—in heaven.

Newbury was founded in 1870, only nine years after the State of Kansas entered the Union. Most of the State, labeled the "great American desert" on early maps, was acquired from France in 1803 as part of the Louisiana Purchase. The early settlers planned Newbury to be the main town in the region because they thought the Santa Fe Railroad would pass through it. Instead, the Santa Fe line bypassed the area altogether. Two years after the parish church was built in Newbury the Rock Island line began to lay its rails westward from Topeka up the Mill Creek valley about two miles south of the church. By 1886 businesses began to relocate from Newbury to an area near the railroad and a new town came into being. It was named Paxico after an Indian medicine man who had lived on the north bank of Mill Creek opposite the old mill. So Paxico became the town and Newbury stayed a village but remained the vibrant center of life for the growing Catholic population.

By the time I was born, the village of Newbury consisted of the church, erected in 1884, the school, built in 1905, the Knights of Columbus Hall, the rectory, the convent and three other nearby houses. Dedicated to the Sacred Heart, the parish church in Newbury had a tall spire and was made of stone. Our pastors had firmly planted within their flock the seeds of love and devotion to the Sacred Heart of Jesus. On the first Fridays of the month everyone possible attended Mass. These were not days of "obligation" but an outpouring of great faith. Through many difficult times of trial and crisis in our family and in the community, I could always hear the prayer: "O Sacred Heart of Jesus, I place my trust in you."

In 1921, the same year my great grandmother Otillia Hund died, the church burned down. We lived then less than a mile south of our parish church. I was six years old and I can still see the flames rising in the sky. It was a First Friday with a larger than usual number of parishioners attending Mass. Without any firefighting equipment, the church burned completely, leaving only a stone walled cavern. It was traumatic for the local population, most of whom were Catholic, and the experience surely put their faith to the test. Sacred Heart Parish was their home. But out of the ruins came a most beautiful twin-spired church, lovingly referred to as the

Sacred Heart Church, built in 1922. It replaced the stone church that burned down the year before. In the view below, Sacred Heart School is on the left and the Knights of Columbus Hall on the right.

"Cathedral of the Flinthills." With its red tile roof and birch limestone trim, the church remains an impressive sight today.

Paxico's population numbered about 200. Main Street had a post office, a hardware store, and a meat market. There was a lumber yard, a bank, a drug store and of course, a blacksmith shop. The big attraction for me was the large Glotzbach Brothers General Store. It had everything: food staples, pots and pans, furniture, kitchen ranges, heating stoves, yardage of every fabric for skillful mothers to sew their children's clothes, including pretty prints for new school dresses,

4

unbleached muslin for "bloomers" (though a lot of them were made from bleached flour sacks), and Oshkosh suspender overalls for men and boys. If all else failed, the Montgomery Ward Mail Order Catalog was always there to the rescue. If someone needed a coffin, good old Glotzbach Brothers could take care of that too, as one of the brothers was the local undertaker and funeral director.

My family, the village of Newbury and the neighboring town of Paxico comprised the world of my childhood—the world that shaped my early dreams and aspirations.

The Meinhardt Farms

My grandparents, August and Frances Meinhardt, had two sons and five daughters. They lived in a lovely home on the land, built by the skill of the early settlers. I fondly remember the "home place" as it was called. This house, where my father was born and raised, was later occupied by his younger brother, my uncle Phillip, his wife Theresa and their family. It had a covered porch with a beautiful wisteria vine clinging to the pillars and the inevitable porch swing for which my siblings and cousins would vie for space. The house had lots of gingerbread, or carpenter art, as did most of the farmhouses built in that era. On the other side of the railroad track was the land that my father farmed, always referred to as the McCrumb Place. I remember the huge slab of flat, white stone that served as a patio. In the cool of a summer evening we would sit and listen to the croaking of the bullfrogs. Some would sing, "knee deep, knee deep." It was quite a chorus, especially after a heavy rain.

Between the two farms, the Rock Island trains traveled east and west bearing carloads of grain, coal, livestock, oil or whatever needed to be transported across the country. We would listen for the rather mournful, though melodic, whistle as we watched from the porch for approaching trains. My brothers and cousins would count the freight cars as they slithered away around the bend. It was the beautiful passen-

The Village of Newbury

Main Street, Paxico

The Town of Paxico

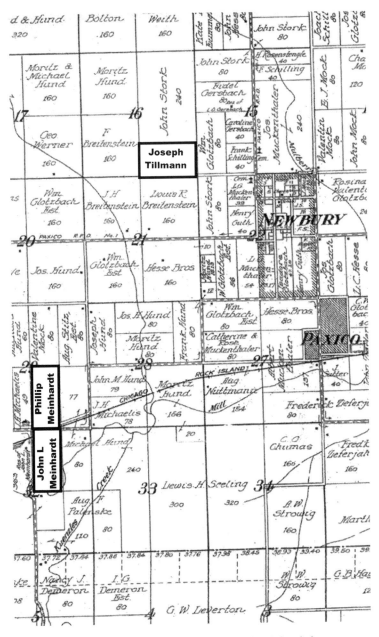

My world: Newbury, Paxico, the Tillmann and Meinhardt farms.

Family photo taken at the "Home Place." Otto, Olga in back, Rita, my dad holding me, Leo and Paul.

ger trains that fascinated me. We could see the passengers seated by the windows, occasionally giving us a wave, as they were swept out of sight. I was only four years old with no experience or understanding of what lay beyond. We didn't have the visual assistance of movies or television to dream of the vastness of an ocean or the grandeur of snowcapped mountains.

With my arrival, it seems to me, my parents' lives were severely changed. It all started with the untimely death of my grandfather, August Meinhardt. He and my grandma were still living in the "home place" and planning to retire to a house they had built in the town of Paxico. They had achieved prosperity from farming the land and feeding cattle, marketing carloads of prime beef, ready for the finest hotels and restaurants in New York. They were enjoying their new automobile, and Grandpa was on his way to visit my parents and see the newborn granddaughter. Crossing the railroad tracks, the car stalled. No one knew for sure what happened. Being a new driver, he may have made a mistake shifting gears. Sadly, the car rolled backwards and crashed into the

The Meinhardt kids in 1916. I'm in the box, next to Paul, then Otto, Leo and Rita.

ditch. A neighbor, driving by with horse and buggy saw the wreck, and got help, but it was too late. Grandpa was pronounced dead at the early age of 62 years on November 17, 1915, a day after my birth.

Grandma, I'm sure, was distraught with anguish and shock. The death of her husband of thirty-five years must have caused her grief, almost too much to bear, but Grandma Meinhardt was a woman of great strength. I feel certain that she accepted this tragedy with courage and resignation, having faced great hardship early in her life. Living with the fear of hostile Indians where she spent her childhood on a homestead in Minnesota, undertaking the long cross-country trek in covered wagons and facing the difficulties of relocating to another state certainly were not for the faint of heart.

The sad news of Grandpa's death quickly spread through the community on the party line "crank" telephones. August Meinhardt was a well-respected man who had prospered as a cattle feeder. In fact, his obituary in the *Kansas City Star* called him a "Kansas cattle baron." He had a reputation as an honest and straightforward gentleman in his dealings in parish and civic affairs. His death was a great shock to the entire community.

Here I am at about 6 months old.

CHAPTER TWO
HARD TIMES ON THE FAMILY FARM

Crisis Time

After Grandma moved into the house in Paxico, Dad's brother, Phillip, purchased the "home place" and my father bought the land adjoining it south of the railroad track. He borrowed the money at an exorbitant rate of interest. Unfortunately, anything that could have gone wrong did go wrong.

For two years my dad fed Hereford, "white face," cattle to prepare them for market. When they were ready for sale he accompanied two carloads of his fatted steers by rail to the Kansas City stockyard. He had promised my mother to bring her a fur piece. Instead, she saw him coming home afoot, carrying no gift box, looking completely dejected. Radios weren't invented yet, so she had not heard the bad news. The livestock market had crashed; there were no takers, no market for his cattle. He had to walk away, leaving the cattle behind. He didn't even bring a couple of them home to butcher.

The following two years my father planted a new grain crop, millet or "cafricorn." Again, he was fortunate to produce a superior crop and anticipated a good return for his labor. He loaded the crop onto two freight cars and once again headed off to market. This time his goods were refused. It had rained somewhere along the way, the grain got wet, and mold grew quickly.

Crisis time! "Papa can't pay the bank; they will take over the farm."

At the time I understood nothing of money but I knew my parents were upset and worried. I was also aware that there was something ominous happening and it was the reason why we have to move.

But that wasn't the first tragedy. Barely a month after I was born, just before Christmas, Grandma Tillmann died. Then, in April 1916, while she was still grieving the loss of her mother, my mother lost her oldest child, Olga, who died of scarlet fever at nine years of age. My mom told me how sad it was for her. They put Olga in a casket, and because scarlet fever was a contagious disease, the family was quarantined. No one could come or go. My dad took the spring wagon with the casket carrying their golden-haired first-born to the cemetery alone. My mother couldn't go because she had to stay home with the children—Rita, Paul, Otto, Leo and me. Before long, Mom became pregnant with Fred. During that

Rita, Olga and Paul. Olga is about six in this picture.

time she suffered a stroke that left her right hand paralyzed. She was 31 years old.

In my maturity I have been able to appreciate what a distressing time that must have been for her. I think her life was one long series of events that might have broken a weaker person, but her deep faith was always her strength. "God's will be done!" Even the move off the farm was seen as a blessing in disguise. I remember how happy they were to enroll their children in the parochial school to be taught by the Benedictine Sisters. Until then, my three oldest siblings, Olga, Rita and Paul, attended school in a one-room country school house.

The Move to Newbury

The house we moved into when we left the farm was less than a mile south of Newbury. It had two bedrooms on the first floor. My sister, Rita, and I shared one. The boys, Paul, Otto, Leo and Fred, occupied the one big room upstairs with a brick chimney in the middle. Their beds were along the four walls.

When Rita finished eighth grade, she left to work for pay in the home of a farm family. She was gone before I entered first grade. On my fourth birthday, Mom delivered a new baby brother, Oscar. I was nearly six years old when Dick arrived. My mother had a struggle his first year because the baby had

The house in Newbury where we lived after the farm.

13

The Meinhardt siblings in 1918: I'm sitting on the chair. The baby is Fred. The others are Otto, Rita, Paul and Leo.

what they called "summer complaint." I'm sure they thought they would lose him. And though I didn't realize it, Mom was already carrying another child. I was almost seven years old, but had not yet been enrolled in school. The spring before, my Dad, Otto, Leo and I were seriously ill with "flu pneumonia." I think the rumor was out that we were all going to die. I remember our pastor coming to give us the last rites. I can see now why I hadn't been enrolled in school. I wasn't strong enough and had lots of attacks of pleurisy. Also, being the only girl at home I can imagine how much my mother needed me to help take care of the little brothers.

In November, ten days after my seventh birthday, little Archie arrived. He was very jaundiced and was not expected to survive. He did, only to be found to be a victim of cerebral palsy. He was completely helpless. He was never able to talk, sit, or even hold his head upright. He had to be spoon-fed. His own hands were useless as he had no control in his arms. During my grade school years it was always my job to feed him. Mom would remind us that "Whatsoever you do for the least of my brethren that you do unto me." So Archie was our little Jesus. His big blue eyes and golden blonde, slightly curly hair and sweet smile made him easy to love.

But he was an enormous amount of work for my mother. Lots of laundry. It was often suggested that he be placed in a Kansas State institution for the disabled, but my Dad would not hear of it. "God gave him to us and it is our duty to take care of him." Even my mother's close-following pregnancy didn't change his mind. Of course at this stage, we were only discovering the extent of Archie's disabilities. As the months went by it was quite evident that he was severely handicapped.

Just two years later another little boy was born very ill—yellow as a daffodil. He was baptized and named Clement Anthony. He lived five days. I remember a neighbor, Henry Guth, farmer and carpenter, made him a pine coffin. Neighbor ladies lined it with white linen and placed a little pillow under his head. He looked so sweet, so peaceful. Someone had brought my mother a narcissus plant, so they decorated the coffin and put a tiny white flower in his yellow hand. All of us—parents, brothers and sisters—stood around him and cried and cried. Momma assured us that the Angels came and took his beautiful innocent little soul to be with Jesus. The room was filled with the scent of the narcissus bloom. I go back to that scene every time I smell a narcissus. At that time, mothers remained bed-fast for ten days after a birth. So once again Dad had to take a child to the cemetery without her, but this time he took the other siblings. I don't remember a Church service. It was winter, December 10, 1923. Our old pastor had just baptized him. I never heard of the "Mass of the Angels" until years later. I wish it could have been celebrated for him and for my sister, Olga.

No matter how difficult the times were, the loss of a child was the greatest cause of grief and sorrow. Today, little baby Clement rests beside his sister Olga, as well as Rita, who lived to age 85, and brother Archie, who died at 35. Baby Marie, a stillborn, sadly, was buried in an unblessed section of the cemetery because she was not baptized. That pathetic rule has been changed, thank God. I think it got derailed on the way to Limbo, which is now a ghost town on the route to Heaven.

My parents firmly believed that God never sends you more than you can bear. I really don't know how they could have borne the many trials and tribulations that came their way without their deep faith that God would give them the strength to bear it.

Eventually, the loss of the farm was complete. Dad had rented the land for a year or more and then fell very ill with double pneumonia. He miraculously passed the crisis at home. The Knights of Columbus provided a nurse and he seemed to be recovering but developed an infection in his lungs. He was then hospitalized in Kansas City for what seemed like a couple of weeks. He finally recovered but was weak and remained in poor health.

I really don't know what the family did for money or where the food came from. In today's emergency times public welfare programs or the St. Vincent de Paul society provide aid to those in need. I think relatives contributed a little food, but I remember it being an impossible time. Dad couldn't farm, so he eventually got a job driving an oil truck that kept him living in the neighboring town during the week. That was not profitable and didn't last very long. There were no jobs for an ex-farmer. He attempted various business ventures and even dabbled a bit in politics, but he never really managed to find the kind of employment required to support such a large and growing family. It was always a struggle.

But hard times require creative solutions, so for a while, my dad and older brothers supplemented the family income by operating a clandestine still, which was illegal under both federal law and a Kansas law that remained in effect long after the repeal of Prohibition. This illicit phase lasted until Dad's cousin, the town banker, got into trouble for selling their wares. Fortunately, no one ever came looking for the still. Of course, I didn't know about that at the time. I just knew we were poor compared to our aunts, uncles and cousins—and the fear of being poor would haunt me for many years to come.

We canned as much garden food and available fruit as we could. We had chickens that produced eggs which we ate or traded in at the grocery store for beans and rice. Flour from the local mill was the most important ingredient. Dad would get 30 bushels of wheat from his brother and take it to the mill in Wamego, a neighboring town, and bring back 50-pound bags of flour. Yeast was always on hand as with each batch of homemade bread some of the starter sponge was stored in a crockery jar. We also had lots of bean soup.

My parents didn't have many pictures taken of their family during my childhood. Only one photo taken of me between 1918 and 1935 exists today, and it is badly damaged. I am about six years of age. The others are Fred, to my left, and Leo, Otto, Rita and Paul.

Our principal meal was at noon. We school kids ran three quarters of a mile home in the noon hour for our midday meal. We didn't like to carry our lunches because we were the only kids who had whole wheat bread. Dad had read somewhere about vitamins and that whole wheat flour was better than white flour. To us kids it was an embarrassment not to have nice white bread. Whether Mom liked or not, she was expected to turn out "good" bread with brown flour. What she made was heavy and moist and actually very similar to what we're buying at specialty bakeries now. So we would come home to bean soup and dark bread, but no one left the table without. "We give Thee thanks O Lord, for these and all the benefits we have received from thy bounty through Christ Our Lord. Amen." I will have to say I secretly questioned this seemingly non-existent bounty. Little did I know how nourishing our fare really was. When the school nurse came to check the students' teeth, not one Meinhardt kid ever had a cavity.

But credit for that should probably be given to that awful rusty-tasting water drawn up in the old oaken bucket from our well. It was very salty and tasted strongly of minerals. We got used to it, but when we had company they would often bring a jug of water from their own well, so they didn't have to drink ours.

A Trip to the Big City

Growing up in rural Kansas I had never seen a city, only a couple of small towns. Some of my classmates had been to Topeka to attend the Kansas Free Fair. My dreams of traveling even that far—only 30 miles away—were a blank slate. I couldn't visualize what I had never been exposed to, but that didn't stop my desire. Sometimes, in fact quite often, I would have dreams of trying to board a train but never getting there before the train started to move down the track huffing and puffing and sending long billowing trails of smoke as it picked up speed and rolled away. Time after time this recurring dream would awaken me and my heart would be pounding as if I had actually exerted all my energy in that effort.

During those years all over Kansas, fifth or sixth grade kids like me were joining "Capper Clubs." Our long-time senator, Arthur Capper, wanted kids to have the experience of joining a group that would foster small agricultural projects, such as raising a batch of chicks, having a pair of rabbits, a pig, or a calf or tending a small garden. Under the supervision of an adult, Capper Clubs provided a little camaraderie, a little competition, a little learning how to organize and conduct a short meeting, and a little playtime together. The experience was fun and wholesome.

The exciting part was to hope your project could be entered in the display at the Kansas Free Fair held on the outskirts of Topeka every September. And you weren't counted absent if you went during the school week! Senator Capper had arranged $1 train tickets for the thirty-mile trip to Topeka. We would travel as a group and a bus would take us to the fairgrounds from the depot. I was so excited at the prospect.

But sad to say, I couldn't go. My parents didn't come up with $1 and a little spending money. I was so crushed I couldn't eat any breakfast that day and went to school knowing that most of my classmates would be absent. On the way to school one of the mothers saw me and asked why I wasn't going to the fair. I didn't want to tell her the reason. I just said, "I can't go."

We school kids attended Mass every day before school began. About halfway through I began to feel faint, so I got up to go outside. I almost made it, but the floor came up to meet me and hit my face. Someone got me back on my feet and took me outside and I sat on the steps to recover.

Just then my older brother, Otto, came driving our Model T up to the Church and saw me sitting there like a forlorn basket case. "Get in the car," he shouted, "Aunt Burgie is going to drive you to the fair." Even if I had expired and rigor mortis

19

had set in, those words would have brought me back to life. His announcement was comparable to my daughter Marge calling me many years later to invite me to accompany her to Africa.

My first trip to the big city. I was so excited when we arrived at the fair grounds and saw so many people in one place. As we made our way through the crowds we heard the band making way for the elephant parade. I had heard about those huge animals but never did I dream that I would see at least 20 of them marching in single file, each elephant's trunk connected to the tail of the one ahead. This was the first part of the Greatest Show on Earth which that year was the fair's "Spectacular Night Show," the Ringling Brothers Barnum and Bailey Circus. Not only did we stay for the night show but we took in some of the side shows. Of course, we saw the bearded lady and other oddities. The barkers at each tent would sway the crowds to enter. I was simply overwhelmed to see a newborn hippopotamus and, of course, his mother. But nothing compared to the dozen of bejeweled girls performing acrobatics on horses and elephants. And I was breathless to see the trapeze artists and the tight rope performers. I could hardly take it all in. My sweet, kind Aunt Burgie gave me one of the best days of my life!

The County Exams

At school we all worked hard at our assignments and at memorizing the catechism. Spelling and catechism got "heard" every night after a session around the long dining table with the kerosene Rayo lamp in the center.

In our combined seventh and eighth grade classroom we were constantly preparing for "county exams." They were very tough and all of us worked very hard to bring honor and maybe even glory to our Catholic school. And indeed, we did, always achieving the highest scores. The results were published in the county newspaper. Imagine the burden on our

Sacred Heart School

teacher, responsible for simultaneously instructing two grades of 25 to 30 students each.

I can remember especially the physiology part of the test. We had to be prepared to draw a diagram of the heart and lungs, the arteries and organs, trace the blood flow, and name all the principal bones of the skeleton and the parts of the brain. Now I see my grandkids studying anatomy for college and I think we were just a step away. We also had to study agriculture, covering all crops, the benefits of diversification, domestic animals—their breeds and characteristics—and anything to do with reaping a harvest and providing food for families and the world. We were required to have wide knowledge of natural resources and the potential of the earth to supply our needs. Spelling, English, history and arithmetic were also covered. We rejoiced when the test was over. Who ever heard of "spring break"?

My mother's sister, Dora, had entered the Benedictine order at their monastery in Atchison, Kansas when she was very young. As a nun she became Sister Antoinette. She always taught grade school but was never allowed to teach at Newbury, her childhood home town. My favorite teacher was my no-nonsense, gifted seventh and eighth grade teacher. I have never forgotten Sister Alphonsina.

Dawn of the Depression

By 1925 I was ten years old and the only girl at home with seven brothers. Baby Archie was about three years old and it was more and more apparent that he would never be able to do anything for himself.

Laundry was an ever present problem. Water for laundry was drawn up from a well in an old oaken bucket and heated on the wood burning cook stove in a big copper boiler. The home made soap made use of lard grease, especially from the second rendering at hog butchering time. The first rendering in a big black kettle over an outdoor fire produced a year's supply of cooking fat. Stored in five gallon crocks, the lard was nice and white and wonderful for cakes, pies and frying potatoes. The dregs from the rendering when mixed with lye became our homemade soap. It was cut into bars and was great laundry soap, but we hardly knew what suds were in that awful "hard" water.

The only soft water was the rain water drained off the roof into a cistern, a large concrete tank, perhaps ten feet deep. It had its own pump—hand operated, of course. This water was used for Saturday evening shampoos and baths together with a ten cent bar of the more gentle Castile soap we could get from the general store.

The next day, dressed in "Sunday best," the family went to morning Mass. We were never all together, though, because someone always had to stay home with Archie. The brothers were all Mass servers. At age ten I was very jealous of them. I couldn't understand why only boys could assist at the altar. From my perspective, girls were only good for being mother's helpers; and with all those brothers, mother needed a lot of help. At this time, once again, Mom was pregnant, and to my great pleasure she delivered a baby girl, named Agnes Theresa. Little Agnes was petite and pretty with pure white hair and blue eyes.

The oldest boy in the family, my gentle, kind, big brother, Paul, wanted to become a priest. This, of course, was a joy to my parents. I think some relatives pitched in to help outfit him for going off to the Benedictine boarding school in Atchison, Kansas, about 100 miles away. We all cried when he left. His departure was a great loss to me, as Paul had been a beautiful part of my early years. I recall with a shudder the most embarrassing moment of my life and the way Paul helped me survive it. One Friday afternoon just as the eighth grade boys were exiting the school building, the elastic waistband of my bloomers disconnected—a "wardrobe malfunction" as Janet Jackson would say—and down came the bloomers tangled around my ankles. I wanted to die! Of course, I cried all the way home and was sure I'd never, ever return to my third grade class again. But, thank God, it was Friday, and by Monday morning my sweet brother Paul had convinced me that not one of the boys was looking my way.

On his visits for the Christmas holidays Paul was eager to share what he was learning. He taught his brothers sports, especially football, had us singing new songs, and trained us to play entertaining new games. He was blossoming. And as a bonus during his holiday breaks we had almost daily dinner invitations from our aunts and uncles.

How I loved the wonderful dinners: goose or duck or large chickens with delicious stuffing. All the produce of the previous summer canning season supplied the bounty: watermelon pickles, dill pickles, pickled peaches, crabapples, wonderful fruit pies, cakes, homemade bread and rolls. All my aunts had lots of daughters to help, whereas my mother only had me and with her poor health and pregnancies we weren't able to produce the delicious meals the other families took for granted. Since we didn't live on the farm anymore we didn't have the variety or quantity of produce for canning the others had—but we did have a storage pit, a deep hole lined with straw, where we stored apples. I remember the Jonathans coming out at Easter time after being buried all winter.

When Agnes was two and a half, Mom had another baby girl, Lucy Antoinette. I was twelve years old. Rita was working for the family of the local druggist as nanny, housekeeper, and cook. Paul continued his studies at Maur Hill, the Benedictine prep school at Atchison. Otto graduated from grade school and because of the family's financial problems he, like Rita, did not enter high school.

Otto worked on my Aunt Burgie's farm where my Grandpa Tillmann also lived. Aunt Burgie was a widow. Her husband had been thrown from a galloping horse and died of complications from a broken neck. She had two daughters, Juanita and Bertha, and two sons, Urban and August. They were off at boarding school, so there were lots of chores for Otto to do: wood to chop and pile, cows to milk and horses to feed. Aunt Burgie, my mother's sister, was a very wonderful and kind lady. I'm sure she was aware of the hard times our family was having and giving Otto a job was her way of helping out.

But Otto should have been in school. It was the time following Dad's bout with pneumonia. If things are darkest before the dawn, it was surely as black as midnight with no guarantee of a dawn in sight. This was a period of day-to-day struggle in our lives. It would be impossible for me to write my life's story without this memory surfacing because it was so very difficult to keep food on the table at that time. Every Sunday the boys went hunting for rabbits and were usually successful. There was a lot of talk about the country being in "depression" and folks who'd always had plenty were forced to sell more and more to make ends meet. Then, in 1929, the New York stock market crash brought the whole country to the realization that we were in real trouble. Banks were failing and President Hoover didn't seem to know what to do about anything.

About this time my Dad was able, somehow, to go into business. He bought eggs and cream from local farmers and sold them to wholesalers in Topeka. He also sold feed and other livestock supplies. For a while it seemed the family was able to count on a little income. Rita quit her job and worked for Dad testing cream, keeping books and whatever there was to do to run the little store.

Otto, Leo and Paul rabbit hunting in 1927.

As difficult as life was then, it wasn't all sadness and tears. One of my favorite childhood memories is about listening to the phonograph, which my mother had purchased from some estate for fifteen dollars. The shelves were filled with great music records of all the great artists of the day: Enrico Caruso, an Italian tenor; Madame Ernestine Schumann-Heink, a great soprano; the Irish tenor, John McCormack and many other opera singers. I learned many arias and loved to sing with the records. I remember reading Poe's "The Masque of the Red Death." It was an eerie story and I had Strauss waltzes playing on the Victrola Gramophone. To this day, I can see that grand ballroom sealed off to protect the high society from the plague while they danced—to the tunes of Strauss waltzes.

During the summer of 1930 our youngest brother was born. He was John Leo Jr. We called him Buddy. He and Agnes and Lucy were the joy of my life. They were very much in my care. I thought they were the cutest, smartest little kids ever. Archie too enjoyed them. At this time, I was approaching graduation and intended to enroll in the public high school. We unexpectedly had a chance to rent a house near the church and school. The house we had been living in had a big country kitchen and no dining room. The new house had a smaller kitchen but a separate dining room, a living room and more bedrooms. It also had a lawn and three big ancient trees in the front yard.

To me, our new place was a gift from God. In summer, we kids slept outdoors because it was too hot to sleep inside. How I loved to sleep under the stars and listen to the nightingale singing and then wake up to the song of wrens, cardinals and other song birds.

Dick, Fred, Oscar, Agnes, Lucy and Buddy, in 1932.

Agnes and Lucy in 1933.

Agnes and Lucy in 1934 with Buddy.

CHAPTER THREE
THE GREAT DEPRESSION

The Academy

In the fall of 1930 I enrolled in Paxico Rural High School along with my other classmates from Sacred Heart School. After a couple of weeks my parents received a letter from my aunt, Sister Antoinette, with an invitation for me to accept a tuition-free academic scholarship to Mount St. Scholastica Academy in Atchison. It was a big boarding school with girls from all over the Midwest, especially Kansas City. The invitation created a big dilemma for my folks. My dad didn't want me to go for reasons I will never understand while my mom wanted me to go even though she was giving up a lot of help. But there was another problem. Not only were they financially unable to outfit me, they couldn't even get me there. Finally, after much arguing, the matter was resolved and they agreed I could go. My cousin Juanita, an alumna of the academy, and her husband came to my rescue by providing me with some supplies and a trip by car to Atchison. It was the farthest away from home I'd ever been and I knew I would miss the kids, but I loved to study and wanted to do it. So I gritted my teeth and headed off with determination.

School had already been in session a couple of weeks when I arrived and all the other girls seemed to have their friends and know their way around. And then I was given my "duties," to earn my board and room. I worked at least an hour before classes and another after scrubbing and scouring drinking fountains, bathrooms and even broom closets. I missed most of recreation and barely made it to study hour. During the evening recreation time, Sister Antoinette would invariably call me to the hall and instruct me on proper behavior and encourage me to think about becoming a sister. Well, I always knew my vocation was to be a mother. I loved kids—even my brothers! No matter how hard it was to maintain our family I still knew they were all precious and that one day we'd "make it."

Meanwhile, back home the Depression was getting worse, the local bank had failed and no one had any money. I got the bad news that I'd have to remain at school during the Christmas holidays because there was no money for a train ticket. I'll have to say this was probably the lowest point in my young life. It came to me in living color: you are poor, poor, poor. I cried myself to sleep and to this day I don't know how it is that I got home, but I did. Paul also got home for the holidays, the last time for years. After finishing high school that year, he gave up his studies for the priesthood and entered the Benedictine Brotherhood.

Mount St. Scholastica Academy

I returned to school after Christmas, but with much trepidation. I was in the infirmary at least five times that year with tonsillitis. The old sister infirmarian would never welcome me because she was so disgusted with me for not having had a tonsillectomy. Well, I was too, but my dad would not give his consent, much to my mother's aggravation. He was convinced I would bleed to death. At that point I really didn't care if I did. I had an average of eight or nine attacks of tonsillitis every school year, complete with chills and fever and delirium. I'd spend at least four days in bed and need two or three more days to get my strength back after a lot of night time "weak sweats." This part of my life is best forgotten, but it was such a large part of my young existence. I lost countless school days from absence due to illness. In seventh grade, I was not in attendance even once for the monthly report card day. So the thought of being able to go to boarding school without having to slosh through mud and snow and freezing temperatures gave me hopes of better health. But even there it caught up with me.

On the last day of school, I was called to the principal's office where I was warmly welcomed by Mother Lucy, the Prioress of the Benedictine Sisters at Atchison. At that time I think they had several hundred sisters. The convent was part of a beautiful complex of buildings. Most of the sisters were on mission during the school year as they were the principal source of supply for many parochial schools all over Kansas, Nebraska, Iowa and Missouri.

Well, back to the principal's office and my very special meeting with Mother Lucy, who had wanted to see me. I was scared—I'd never met her. But she greeted me with a hug and invited me to finish my high school education at Mount St. Scholastica Academy. I thanked her. I was really overcome, because I didn't have a chance of continuing at the Mount unless it was free.

But I was not to return for the fall term. "You are needed at home," was the verdict from my parents. The following two

29

years I lived in limbo. There was no doubt that I was needed at home but I often question myself why I didn't fight at least to go back to the local high school.

During 1934, my Dad was having heart trouble. Not only was the Depression in full misery but the drought was burning up every last green leaf and blade of grass. Trees were dying and the gardens dried up for lack of rain. Dust storms were frequent, frightening, and a new experience for us. The sun would hang in the reddish brown sky like a bright ball while a fine, gritty dust filtered its way into our homes through every crack, covering floors, furniture, bedding, utensils— everything. Fortunately, during this period Dad was able to get work as a timekeeper through the WPA, President Roosevelt's program to employ people to build roads, dams, parks, etc. It was only temporary, but for the Meinhardts, the job was a lifesaver.

St Marys

When I was seventeen, the opportunity came for my sister and me to be employed in St. Marys, a town only fifteen miles away, but with a very different environment. It was a college town with a population of 1,200 and a higher level of education than most rural communities. The parish there served a very large rural population. Rita found work in a creamery and I got a job on a farm as housekeeper and cook.

After Rita and I had left our home in Newbury, the severity of the drought increased to the point that the term "Dust Bowl" became the new name for Western Kansas. The small business that my dad was operating had to close. The "cream station" in Paxico could no longer operate because the cows had no green pastures. As a result, the farmers didn't have cream to sell. Egg and chicken production diminished for the same reason. Most families used their produce for their own table rather than sell it. So the business folded and the family moved to St. Marys.

With my sister Rita, 1935.

Rita and I had found a house to rent on a nice shaded street for $10.00 a month, and wonder of wonders, we purchased a washing machine and an electric radio! This was our first experience with a time payment plan and a home with electricity, although it did not have indoor plumbing. It was 1934.

So the family settled in. The youngest kids—little sisters Agnes and Lucy and brother Buddy—were enrolled in the parish school. Dick, ready for high school, was accepted into the former all girls' high school as the first co-ed student. Two others, brothers Fred and Oscar, went to the public high school and Otto and Leo worked various jobs, running newspaper routes, delivering groceries, mowing lawns or whatever little jobs were available, Mother was home with our little brother, Archie. Rita worked at the St Marys creamery and I was at the Doyles.

The Doyles

The Doyles were Black Angus cattle feeders. Mr. Doyle and son Leo did the farming. Mr. and Mrs. Doyle were highly regarded in the community. The farm was located about two miles west of town. A creek ran through the land. A stone wall hid the cattle from view and a big red barn sheltered the horses and stored grain and hay. Leo's 1933 Chevrolet, which he had won at the parish bazaar, was also stored there.

The drought was creating overwhelming problems for farmers. The corn crops failed and on top of that there was a grasshopper invasion. Standing near a cornfield one could hear a low-pitched buzz as thousands of grasshoppers chewed on the cornstalks. At last, the battle was lost and Mr. Doyle had to surrender to the insects. The cornfields were cut down and the remaining stalks gathered for fodder. But it wasn't enough. Grain had to be purchased to finish the cattle feeding that season. It would be an understatement to say it was not a profitable year for him.

Then, dear Grandma Doyle had a stroke and was confined to bed. I took care of her the last three months of her life. At first, a practical nurse looked after her. Part of her job was to teach me how to attend to a bedridden patient. So I got the care-giving duty in addition to cooking, cleaning, washing, ironing, churning butter, baking bread, etc.

After her death it might have been a good time for me to move on, especially since I was there with only Mr. Doyle and son Leo. But the choices were limited and the monthly check was crucial to my family's support. So I stayed on. After Mrs. Doyle passed away the workload eased and I was a little more

The drought of the 1930s caused hardship for Kansas farmers.

comfortable with being the main housekeeper with all its duties—some of which I hated. Washing a cream separator was not my idea of fun and it had to be done nightly. But the butter was plentiful and delicious. Sometimes there was enough to trade in for other groceries. Since there was no rural electrification at that time butter had to be hand churned. In the summer we got blocks of ice for an ice chest to keep the milk and butter cold. Meat consisted mostly of cured hams and smoked bacon. Through the years I probably cooked more casseroles of scalloped potatoes topped with bacon strips from the smokehouse than the army did, but the Doyles never tired of the fare and I learned that one doesn't need fresh meat every day.

On Monday mornings, laundry days, Mr. Doyle would fill the big copper boiler with water he had pumped and carried in to heat on the coal and wood range. He also helped me with pumping the washing agitator stick back and forth. Then I put the clothes and linens through the hand turned wringer into the rinse. After soaking in a tub of clean water, the clothes went through the wringer again and then into the clothes basket to be hung on the clothes line to dry in the wind and sun. In winter the laundry would freeze stiff as a board as I pinned the underwear, work clothes, towels and bed sheets to blow-dry in the wind. Nothing smells so fresh and clean as freeze dried sheets. It all sounds quite primitive, but it was better than doing washing by hand on a scrub board in a tub of cold suds.

Next, I did the ironing, and after that I found time to do some reading. I always had a good book that Leo provided for me. He was a graduate of St. Marys College and had gone on to Marquette University in Wisconsin to get a post-graduate degree in journalism. Like many promising young people at the time, the Depression changed the course of his life. The Catholic daily he edited had to fold for lack of paid subscriptions. He came back to the farm to help his dad with the farming and cattle feeding. Leo Doyle stayed there for the rest of his life and never returned to his profession. While I worked there he demonstrated concern that I had dropped out of school and in a very kind way encouraged my self-education, becoming something of a mentor to me.

Life in the country was peaceful and I was treated with respect and perhaps love. It was there that I determined to improve myself in different ways, especially my health, my spiritual life, and my mind. One thing important to me was missing, however: music. At my home we had lots of music. The Doyles had a piano which did nothing for me since I couldn't play, but I sang all the popular tunes I knew.

We'd had a radio in our house from the time I was in the third grade when my Dad acquired the concession for selling radios. Our first one had earphones. That was not very satisfactory as we had to take turns to listen. Later on, we advanced to a radio with a big, loud speaker and a heavy battery that had to be taken to town periodically to be recharged. As the years went by listening got easier. We tuned into to "Your Hit Parade" every Saturday evening and learned every new song. I loved the "Big Bands" and couldn't wait until I was old enough to learn to dance.

Newbury had a number of musically talented people. The original German population started a marching band and a choir at church. Later, someone organized a dance orchestra. When my mother and dad were young the dance music was mostly fiddle and accordion for square dancing. But when round dancing became popular, the music changed to accommodate ballroom favorites like the waltz and fox trot. During the "flapper" days, when the Charleston was the rage, the shocked traditionalists resisted the change. Eventually, however, jazz became popular and ushered in the Swing Era.

When I was about 14 or 15 I was allowed to attend the dances held in the spacious Knights of Columbus Hall. All the young folks were there. We didn't have to have a date to attend. The young girls would be seated around the perimeter of the dance floor and the guys would congregate in a far corner.

With a friend, 1936.

We girls would watch to see who was approaching, hoping someone would choose us. Soon after the music began and the floor was moving with couples the girls were so eager to dance they'd pick a girlfriend. It was hard to sit still. Eventually, we began to be asked the treasured question, "May I have this dance with you?" My brothers had orders from headquarters to dance with their sisters and then there were all of those young cousins who were just learning. Many the scuffed up shoes from missteps, but that too improved with time and practice. In those days it was essential to invent our own fun. In the heart of the Great Depression entertainment had to be free. Come to think of it, the Great Depression had no heart!

When I moved away, I did miss those events, but soon some of my favorite relatives and friends began to find their way to St. Marys and we often went dancing on Sunday evenings. I had Sunday afternoons off at the Doyles, but not before cooking noontime dinner for Grandpa Doyle, his daughter and her family, who always came home with him after Sunday Mass. Once the dishes were done, Leo would take me to my parents' home. If I had a dime I could just make it to the matinee. I loved the movies. We didn't have a theatre in Paxico, so I was quite happy for the chance to go to the movies.

I was still struggling with tonsillitis at the Doyles. So when I was nineteen years old, now living away from home, I decided to take matters into my own hands. I made an appointment with the local doctor to remove my tonsils. I was sick and tired of being sick and tired. In the German culture that I grew up in the word "rest" did not exist, except for the advice to go to bed early to prepare for the next day's duties. My dad had continued to refuse permission for a tonsillectomy, but once I left home I knew it was time and I was determined to have it done.

But the tonsillectomy was almost a disaster. The doctor said my tonsils were embedded. The Novocain wasn't very effective and it took double the time anticipated. I spent a few days recovering at home with high hopes of becoming stronger and healthier. Then, back to my job in the country. I was still satisfied to be at the Doyles, now no longer having bouts of tonsillitis. I enjoyed the peace and quiet and spent every spare hour reading. I always attended early Sunday Mass with Leo, and returned to cook Sunday dinner with a goal of making it to the two o'clock matinee. Rita, on the other hand, used her day off work to scrub and clean the family home and would be upset with me for my lack of cooperation. At that point in history housework was women's work. I didn't see it that way. I refused to change and make beds for my able-bodied brothers.

But there was no limit to the effort of my sister. Rita was determined to prove to herself and any visitors that the Meinhardt family had a spotless, clean house. No sacrifice of time or pleasure was too much for her. She was driven! My mother had all she could handle with cooking and caring for the smaller kids and Archie. I'm sure she felt guilty or embarrassed that she wasn't able to get all the tasks done. By the time the two little sisters were old enough to help, some of the brothers had left home. But the girls didn't get off the hook. Rita was still in charge of neatness and order and I was enjoying the peace and quiet of the country in the Doyle home a couple of miles out of town.

By 1936 things were getting better for the Meinhardt family in St Marys. My dad was finally able to contribute to the family's support. He rented a greenhouse and garden plot from St. Marys College for a vegetable growing enterprise with hopes of a great return. The beginning of that venture was not auspicious, however. He needed a horse to pull the walking plow and with the help of my brothers found a swaybacked, half-starved horse for $30 to be paid off when the garden produced. They promptly bought bales of hay and oats for the old nag, and the next day were shocked to find she had died—probably of overeating. I'd heard of people having to pay for a dead horse; suddenly, we all learned what that feels like! Eventually, Dad's effort was successful, even without the horse. My dad and brothers produced a great harvest of vegetables—beans, corn, salad greens, tomatoes and much more—for sale and for the family table.

Meanwhile, the family housing situation also improved. An old stone home, one block from Immaculate Conception Church in St. Marys, had sat vacant for much of the Depression. Who but the Meinhardt family could give new life to those walls? With lots of bedrooms and its proximity to school and church, it was just what we needed. The rent was $12 a month.

The stone "mansion" in St Marys.

CHAPTER FOUR
JOHNNY SCHULER

Johnny

I knew about John Schuler long before we met. I heard about him every Sunday when Florence Pearl and her family would come to dinner at the Doyle's. Grandpa Doyle loved to hear his daughter bring news of the Sandy Hook farmers, most of whom were old timers and members of the Catholic community. The name Johnny Schuler would come into conversation—always with respect and admiration. Since I did not know him by sight, I had no idea that the dapper young man who often managed to kneel beside me at the Communion rail on Sunday morning was this ambitious young farmer.

A girl friend loved to talk about her cousin, Johnny. She obviously was very fond of him and promised to introduce him to me, but it never happened. I decided either she really didn't want him to meet me or neither of us was eager enough to plan it. My social life was almost non-existent, except for Sunday night dancing. I felt like an outsider. I wasn't meeting anyone in my new parish until I went to the annual parish bazaar and at last I met my friend's cousin, Johnny. It was unavoidable. I thought he was very nice and I observed that he was a neat dresser. He was wearing a leather sport jacket over a plaid shirt, nicely creased slacks and well-polished brown shoes. I think I was wearing a crocheted dress. My Aunt Mary Zeller had crocheted it for me in a pretty shade of blue.

I loved it. It was a rare gift for me, as I didn't have much of a wardrobe. So, we chatted a while and had some refreshments. When my ride back to the farm arrived, we unceremoniously said goodnight. This was November, 1935. I didn't hear from him until May, 1936. He told me later he got the impression I had a boyfriend, probably because I talked about going to the Sunday night dances. I was only hoping he would want to go too. What he didn't know was that the boys I danced with from Newbury were mostly my cousins. I had a couple of dates, very forgettable to say the least, with my brothers' friends. I was not looking for romance at that time.

At last I got a phone call. Surprise, surprise! It was Johnny Schuler calling and he wants to ask me for a date. How would I like to see a movie? So, we made a date for Memorial Day, May 30, 1936. It was not a day off for me so Johnny came to the Doyle home to pick me up. I was quite impressed with his neat appearance. It was a lovely, warm spring evening and lots of flowers were in bloom. On the way to the car he picked a rose, put the stem through a buttonhole of my new white linen suit. We seemed to be off to a good start. He had a brand new 1936 Ford V 8 Coupe and it had a radio! Nice touch. Then we drove to the next town and saw a musical. I have forgotten the name, but not the music, which included a quartet singing, "All Aboard! On the Atchison, Topeka and the Santa Fe." He was a very proper gentleman and I enjoyed the entire evening.

Of course, we made another date and another and another. We got to know each other and I had nothing but admiration for him, but I wasn't sure about being in love with him. I think my dream of romance had something to do with someone who could sing like Frank Sinatra and maybe play the piano. This Johnny Schuler couldn't carry a tune in a bucket!

He made no secret that he was in love with me and would do everything in his power to win my heart. Maybe I thought he was too good to be true. His sister, Regina, had married a farmer and had four beautiful little girls and a baby boy. I had

seen this family at church and they affected me in the same way. "That's what I want." That much I knew, but something was holding me back. I was afraid I was not up to the task. Still, I enjoyed the rest of the summer.

It was a happy time for both of us. We took lots of drives in different directions. I had some exploring to do because I still felt new to the area. The house on Main Street where my folks lived had a nice lawn and we often spent Sunday afternoons there playing croquet. My dad was most approving of this young man. Johnny lived about six miles out of town and farmed some three hundred acres of corn, wheat and alfalfa. His mother lived with him. I observed that Johnny was always mindful of her and made sure she wasn't alone on Sundays. Our date usually ended with supper at my folks' and an early movie; then he would return me to the Doyles' home.

We put a lot of miles on his new car which was his pride and joy. His godmother who had always been good to him had passed away. She actually willed her home in Kansas City's Plaza District to him, but also listed designated gifts to his cousins. He was to get what was left over after the house was sold. As it turned out, houses were so devaluated during the Depression that the sale brought in so little there wasn't enough to cover the designated gifts of cash. However, Johnny got enough shares of stock to buy his dream, a brand new car—and we were certainly enjoying it.

As time went on and we learned to know each other, it didn't matter that he couldn't sing like Frankie or dance like Fred Astaire. I saw in him every good quality I'd want in a husband: a good Catholic, a man with Jesuit-inspired values who promised to be the best provider he could be, a man who had high hopes in spite of struggle. Above all, he wanted and would treasure a family. And, he was in love with me.

I did question his vision because he thought I was beautiful. No one had ever even hinted as much to me. In fact, I was quite convinced that I was the plainest Jane alive. The mole in the middle of my left cheek, which appeared at the age of 14 or so, clinched it. Like any young teenager I was not happy with my features, especially my hair. It was so unlike my sister Rita's beautiful golden blonde, Agnes's platinum, or Lucy's gorgeous red and wavy hair; mine was dishwater blonde—and straight! I let it grow long (totally out of style) and wore it in a bun. When it got too heavy, I braided it and wound it over my head. Johnny liked that too.

I felt very comfortable with him and he with me. When I first knew him he sometimes had a problem with a stutter. At first I worried about it but realized that when he was relaxed and in comfortable company it didn't happen. I thought if his peers in the community accepted it to the extent of electing him Grand Knight of the local Council of the Knights of Columbus, I would not let it bother me. He had so many good qualities.

I think I made a conscious decision to accept his proposal of marriage with the thought that he would be a wonderful father to my kids. Then, I panicked a week later and tried to tell him I just wasn't ready. He was broken hearted and said he would move away because we wouldn't be able to live in the same community. I suddenly realized I didn't want to lose him and all the beautiful things about him. So we became engaged. I felt confident that this is what was in God's plan for me—and for him.

The recollection of my engagement is a little vague. I don't remember the exact date of my promise to marry John Schuler but we set the date to be married for January 20, 1937. In those times weddings were not necessarily held on a Saturday. In a farming community one weekday was as good as another. Sunday was a day of rest and church, but not for weddings. Neither was the season of Lent. Johnny hoped we could be married before Lent while his work load was lightest. So, a winter wedding was planned. I terminated my job at the Doyles in December and moved home for the month preceding our wedding.

When we became engaged in early November 1936, Johnny was not prepared to give me a ring, but on December 24th he called to see if I was free to go with him somewhere. I forget the pretext he gave, but off we went. We drove north out of St. Marys to the highest hill where "on a clear day, you could see forever." We parked and I could see he was excited. He took my hand in his and with a promise to love me and care for me forever he slipped a ring on my finger. Now, it was official. I too made a promise and God willing our dreams would come true and things get better—"things" being the economy and the weather which had caused a lot of havoc with drought, floods, hail and wind storms. Also, I knew I needed better health for the life of a farmer's wife. So, we put our trust in God and asked His blessing.

Our family traditionally had our Christmas celebration on Christmas Eve. This year we also celebrated our engagement as I proudly showed off my diamond ring.

A Very Special Day

Because of the economy, it would be a simple wedding. Our pastor suggested we be married mid-week at the daily Mass, which was attended by the school children. Ordinarily, that would have been just fine for our guests to attend. Farmers

The formal wedding portrait.

are accustomed to starting the day early. However, the day before our big day there was an ice storm. All the roads were covered with a sheet of ice. Complications! The bridegroom, who lived six miles out of town, worried he wouldn't make it in the morning. Cars were in ditches, skidding and sliding. I thought we could make room for him. There were a lot of bedrooms in the house. Not when my Dad heard about it. "No way! He is not sleeping under the same roof before the wedding." Reluctantly, I had to call Johnny to tell him my Dad did not think it "proper." Why did that not surprise me? We were brought up with so much emphasis on "reputation" and "what will people think?" Well, I had a few thoughts about them! Fortunately, a friend in town offered hospitality for the night. Johnny first took his mother to spend the night at his sister's home.

Next morning, he arrived in time to see me descend the stairs in my pretty $14 satin wedding dress from the Lerner Shop in Topeka and my bridal veil of tulle, which a friend of my mother had fashioned for me. We walked the short distance to the church. The sun was shining, the ice was melting and my feet were getting wet in my pretty satin sandals. Most of my relatives from Newbury, fifteen miles away, were afraid to drive the trip on the icy road and were conspicuous by their absence. Fortunately, some of my favorite aunts, cousins and, of course, my parents and siblings were present—except my dear brother Paul—as were all of the school children.

My sister Rita was my maid of honor and John's cousin, Leo Kramer, was his best man. My brothers were altar boys. There were no other attendants. It was indeed a simple wedding. My girl cousins from Paxico were mostly employed in Topeka, and I had not made close girl friends in St. Marys so I had no other bride's maids. In St. Marys I still felt I was an outsider, but it was not important to me. I had the most important person in the world there who would vow to love me and care for me "until death do us part." He was beaming with pride and joy, looking very handsome in his dark blue tailor-made suit and I was proud to meet him at the altar. This was a very special day. I was at last allowed to enter the sanctuary during our Nuptial Mass. Rita and I on the left side and Johnny and Leo on the right. I say "at last" because I was always envious of my brothers because they were altar boys and were permitted to assist the priest at Mass, while girls were not. We took our vows at the foot of the altar and Johnny solemnly put the wedding ring on my finger. A family friend sang Schubert's Ave Maria and the organist went all out as we walked out to begin our new life as man and wife.

Outside my parents' home after the wedding in the snow, January 20, 1936.

We returned to my parents' house where a lovely breakfast was served to the four of us, as we had been fasting. The guests assembled in the living room and the bridal party made a quick trip to the photo studio. At noon Johnny's mother, his sister and family, my parents and all my siblings sat down to dinner. In all, there were about thirty people there. I think they put two dining tables together, the full length of the dining room. The house was a big old stone mansion with large rooms, a nice entry hall, and an open staircase. I never really got to live there but it made me happy to have our wedding reception there.

The dinner was delicious and served on "Depression glass" loaned by a friend. A neighbor lady cooked the food with help from a couple of friends. Johnny's sister supplied the chicken, and the salads magically arrived at the door. Both Rita and Mom had made lots of friends in St. Marys. Working in the local dairy store, Rita had made the acquaintance of most of the townspeople on her monthly collection route for the milk customers, and my mother made friends at our parish church. They all seemed willing to help.

Somehow, like the miracle of the loaves and fishes, this reception for which we had no money turned out very well. The Great Depression taught us a few lessons in kindness and helping one another. The wedding cake was beautiful, also baked by a friend and neighbor. There were only a few gifts to open: a couple of tablecloths, some silverware and a carving set. My dear Aunt Burgie had made a tulip quilt which I treasured. I did not have a "hope chest." I think I was supposed to have been embroidering pillowcases and tea towels instead of reading books. In any case I came quite empty handed. Johnny's mother and sister gave us a wonderful gift: two home grown and homemade goose down pillows. Even now, after 74 years, I have the remains of their gift in a single, small down pillow.

At about three o'clock we departed for a short honeymoon. We went to Kansas City where the ice was thicker and even more treacherous than in St. Marys. We returned to the farm a couple of days later. Johnny's mother was there alone. I think it had been a struggle for her to keep the fire going. In the bitter cold the house was like an icebox. Not exactly a romantic entry into my first home with my bridegroom. But soon he had the stone fireplace functioning with wood and coal. We were glad to be home, and I think we saved his mother from a very, very cold night.

The next day her move back to her little house in St. Marys began. She had bought it when Regina and Johnny were high school age. It was only a couple of blocks from St. Marys College, close for Johnny as a day scholar and handy for the Jesuit Fathers who kept her busy keeping their clericals in repair. I often thought how dreary it must have been for her

Our first home–a farmhouse with running water.

to work on black wool day after day. Now she would be able to enjoy her little house in retirement. Living in town she'd be able to play cards with friends and be only a block away from the church so she could participate in annual parish dinners, bazaars, picnics, etc. These were big events for a predominately Catholic community. It took most of the first week to get her moved from the farm and settled into her retirement. Only then could Johnny and I begin to make the farmhouse into "our" home.

One of the first projects for Johnny was sinking a pipe into the ground and installing a basin with a small hand pump. *Voilà*, we had water in the kitchen! In the Kaw River Valley there is a wonderful thing called an aquifer, a flow of water underground and it was good water. What a blessing for me. Yes, Johnny would keep his promise of making every effort to make life as good as possible. I had never lived in a house with indoor plumbing so even a pump in the kitchen was wonderful to me. I think one could say I was not spoiled. I was grateful for any little thing that was better than what I had known.

CHAPTER FIVE
THE FARMER'S WIFE

The Farm, 1937

The bitter cold, snow, ice and howling winds whistling through the barren trees, rattling the windows on stormy nights in winter had finally calmed. Slowly the frozen ground yielded to the sun's warming rays. The wheat fields were greening like a verdant spring lawn; calves were dropping from fat pregnant cows, wobbling on shaky legs ready to nurse; baby chicks were thriving; busy robins were building nests and swallows returning from their winter getaway.

Soon it was corn planting time and my farmer was up very early, out in the field laying open long straight rows of rich brown earth to prepare them for the bright yellow kernels of corn. We had high hope that these kernels would produce a rich marketable crop for tables in the city, fodder for the cows in the country, and income for us.

My husband was full of energy and enthusiasm; his spirit connected to nature and the miracle of spring which brings about birth and new growth. He wanted to share every aspect of the work with me. If his tractor had included a passenger seat he would have wanted me there by his side.

Spring, it is confirmed, I am expecting our first baby! Johnny is overjoyed and I am scared.

I knew so little about having a baby. I was fourteen when the last sibling was born in my own family. The baby was due in

The Meinhardt family together on the day of Buddy's First Communion, shortly after we were married.

July when all the children were home. Suddenly we were all scattering before the midwife arrived. I was told to get my brothers and sisters ready to go to my Aunt Burgie's farm for a few days for whatever reason. In those times having a baby was all secret, they were found under a cabbage leaf, or the stork brought them. Today it is common to share the experience of childbirth with family, taking pictures of the birth, cutting the umbilical cord and making it a family celebration. At least I had the hope of delivering my first born in the nearest hospital about twenty miles away. My mother had no choice but home delivery and ten days of "confinement."

In spite of all the chores to be done and the morning sickness, we managed to get the garden planted by the end of April. By that time I was feeling better and beginning to dream of the little son or daughter that was developing in my fast burgeoning belly. Johnny was an only son and had no male Schuler cousins so he was hoping for a boy.

Rapidly the garden was sending forth crispy fresh lettuce, bright red radishes, and rows of perky green onions, dark spinach and chard. We were looking forward to sweet fresh peas and wonderful sun ripened tomatoes.

Before long it was hog butchering time, a typical spring farm activity in which all the neighbors had a major hand—because soon it would be their turn to need help. A big iron kettle strung between two posts over a roaring fire received the trimmings of fat to be rendered for lard. The lard was then stored in five gallon jars in the cool cellar. For the next year we didn't have to worry about having enough for frying chicken or making pies.

Summer came on rapidly that year and the warm weather hastened the ripening of the fruit. Suddenly, we had a bumper crop of peaches, plums, pears and tomatoes needing to be canned. In rural households winter meals always depended on summer preservation. That year the tomato patch was a sight to behold: big juicy, bright red tomatoes ripening in the sun. I'd fill two bushel baskets with them and in less than an hour boil enough water to sterilize the jars and scald the tomatoes. For the other fruit, I had to peel, core or pit it. After being placed in the jars, the next step was to cover the fruit with liquid, exhaust the air and tighten the lids. I would then lower the jars into a copper boiler filled with water and simmer them for a predetermined time depending on the type of fruit, and finally lift them out to cool and finish sealing. It was hard work, but the result was stunning. The jars filled with the colorful fruit looked as beautiful as an artist's painting and I was pleased to show off my display of nearly two hundred quarts of peaches, plums, pears and tomatoes.

The Threshing Crew

The time was drawing near for threshing. Cooking for the crew hired to help with the wheat harvest that year would be a first for me. For several days two dozen men would expect a main meal at noon and supper in the evening. Preparing this dinner was a big challenge for me, but I was determined to do my best and make Johnny proud.

On the first day, I drove the six mile trip to town to the meat market where the butcher advised me about how much meat was needed. Of course, I didn't have a clue because I had never even handled a large roast. I believe I bought most of a hind quarter. The next item to purchase was a very large block of ice for the quantities of lemonade and iced tea the men would consume. Then I headed home. Before I left in the morning, I had already baked four pies from canned fruit. My helper on that nerve-racking day was my mother-in-law. She was a great cook but there was no time to conduct a cooking school. I was on a dead run the entire day, cooking huge pots of potatoes, setting tables, and dealing with a myriad of details before the men came in for dinner at noon.

Basins placed on a bench outside the kitchen door allowed the men to wash up and shake the dust off before dinner. Most of them poured water over their heads to cool off and groom their hair. The dinner turned out well. The meat was perfect and there was more than enough, as is expected when you feed the threshers. Of course, the women did all the work. I can't recall a single man offering to help. Men just did not do this in 1937. Johnny often said that he could not boil water. There may have been a few men who helped their wives but farmers did the outside work and women did the inside work.

Now that the first big dinner was over, the next task to be accomplished was the cleanup, followed by resetting the tables for supper, which would be a lighter meal, mostly leftovers. At four o'clock we took jugs of lemonade to the crew. Why they could not drink fresh water from the well was beyond my understanding.

It was all about "Tradition" as was sung in the play "Fiddler on the Roof." There was a great deal of tradition in the threshing activities, an important annual farming event. I completed five days of this cooking frenzy; two and one-half days for our harvest and the same for our nearest neighbor. The carrot he offered me was one hundred dollars if I would cook for his crew. In those days that was a lot of money.

The unfinished Mount Rushmore we saw in 1937.

The Vacation

After the harvest that first summer of our married life, we did what hardly anyone was able to do since the crash of 1929 and the Great Depression set in. We took a vacation! We had three weeks to do what had only been a dream. Neither of us had been more than a couple of counties away from home, I to Kansas City to the east and I think Johnny had visited his cousins in Hays, in Western Kansas. We both wanted to see a mountain. We also wanted to see a lake. Movies and stereoscope pictures gave us a glimpse of the beautiful world beyond Kansas and a keen desire to see it in reality.

We had Johnny's new car and we were ready to explore the world—and we loved every minute of it. Even now at age 95, I love to drive on a road I have never seen before. It still excites me to cross new mountains and rivers, prairies and deserts, lakes and streams. Bless the Lord. God's beautiful world awaits us.

We traveled north. Our first destination was Mount Rushmore, South Dakota. There had been a lot of interest in the enormous undertaking of sculpting the four faces of past presidents in the mountain top. The sculptor, Gutzon Borglum, had been a professor at St. Marys College, so he was known locally.

In Nebraska as we traveled parallel to the telephone line on a long straight stretch of highway we encountered a severe electrical storm. The clouds were low and black in midday. Suddenly we were in a cloudburst and a blinding flash of lightening struck, followed instantly by the big boom of thunder. In all my life in the Midwest where thunderstorms are common, this was the closest bolt I had ever experienced. We prayed and stepped on the gas pedal as we thanked God that we had not been cremated.

So far our plan for cheap shelter was working. We could drive into a camp for a small fee, pitch a tent, light up the gasoline camp stove, heat up canned stew or pork and beans or whatever we could get at the grocery store. Our car provided our bed. The back seat rest swung upward and the front seat flattened to connect with the back seat. It wasn't the Hilton but we were tourists seeing the sights! Johnny was 30 years old and I was 21.

We headed through the Badlands, miles and miles of sandy hills that had been hewn by the wind into fantastic shapes— an incredible sight—and then we experienced the thrill of seeing Mount Rushmore. It was exciting to drive into the Black Hills. Never before had we seen a forest, only in story books. We continued to travel west until off in the distance loomed real mountains silhouetted against the sky. This was our first look at a major mountain range, this one called the Big Horns. We had no idea about how we would travel over them to get to Cody, Wyoming where we would find the east entrance to Yellowstone Park.

We had seen many pictures of Old Faithful and read about it in geography books, but we didn't have a clue about the enormity and beauty of Yellowstone Park with all its thermal activity. We would sit for hours waiting for certain eruptions until at last they came into full power and shot their steaming fountains to incredible heights and widths. We spent six days camping in different areas, visiting with folks from all across America. Kansas was our world and a very limited part of it. I now had my first taste of travel, my first taste of liberation.

Yellowstone Lake, what a beautiful sight. We watched returning fishermen with silvery trout cleaning their catch while the seagulls feasted. It didn't take us long to rent a boat and equipment and try our luck. The nerve of us. I'm midterm pregnant. Neither of us had ever been in a row boat and couldn't swim, and I'm not sure they provided life jackets. But we were fishing in Yellowstone Lake. And catching fish!

We were hooked. Dusty, dry Kansas just went down the drain. The verdant Kansas of my childhood was no more. We had experienced a severe drought that had killed and blown away all that was comforting—shade trees, green pastures, flowing creeks and even the Kansas River. So at this stage we were simply thrilled to see green forests, lakes, crystal clear water in streams where elk and buffalo could drink and be cool. And my "wannabe" sportsman husband was simply falling in love with the great outdoors. The scenery was so spectacular we hated to leave.

We then traveled south to Estes Park, high in the Rocky Mountains of Colorado. So high in fact the road rises above the tree line. We witnessed another electrical storm, this one way down in the valley below. What a sight. Dizzy from the height and just plain scared, I was glad when we returned to greener pastures. We made it safely through the mountain passes to Denver and Colorado Springs, seeing their red rock formations just as we had viewed them on the stereoscope.

At last we headed east to Kansas. We stopped in Hays to visit Johnny's uncle, Joe Kramer. He farmed a lot of land and had some oil wells pumping in the fields. Joe and his wife had four daughters and two sons. The conversation was about the weather, the crops, the prices—strictly their life on the farm.

More than seven decades later, two of Joe's daughters still have the farm and garden. We exchange greetings at Christmas and I still get the rundown on their weather and farm conditions. Such good people, still caring for family.

We then headed home.

The First Child

When I left I didn't look very pregnant but three weeks later I had gained weight: it's no longer a secret that I am expecting a baby. This will be my parents' first grandchild and my grandma's first great grandchild. Everyone is excited about this—and I am excited. I always dreamed of being a loving mother of beautiful, talented children who would love me and make me proud. But as a teenager, I began to worry that it couldn't happen. When I was nearing sixteen I was skinny and flat as a beanpole and still waiting for the onset of a menstrual period, I feared I was abnormal. Since my First Communion I had been trying to complete the Nine First Fridays, but failed time after time because of a sick spell. So as a teenager I began again to carry out this devotion to the Sacred Heart of Jesus. I placed my trust in Him and prayed for better health.

My first baby was due in early December but for some reason he didn't arrive till December 19. I spent my first Christmas of married life in the hospital in Wamego. My husband was so thrilled with his little son he made the 50-mile trip every day to see us. His first gift to our baby was not a teddy bear, but a living, breathing, fuzzy black bundle of love, a puppy! I was introduced to this talented little sheep dog when I arrived home with my baby son on the tenth day. Unfortunately, I had to remain a few more days in bed, still healing from a difficult birth.

My baby son had decided "none of this 'head first' business for me, I'm going to walk out." Breach births are no fun at all. The doctor had tried unsuccessfully to correct the position and gave up. He decided to leave the hospital for a little while, when suddenly I was in serious labor and being given ether for a total knockout. I heard the nurses calling the doctor to come back, "the umbilical cord and the feet are showing." The result was a torn birth canal, a lot of repair work and a lot of pain. But we have a beautiful little son, John Paul, whom we called Jack. It didn't take long to determine that he needed more nourishment than I could give him. He welcomed the formula in a bottle and thrived. I had him on a very strict schedule and he was a very happy baby.

And the puppy knew the baby was his long before the baby knew the puppy was his.

Counting Chickens

The second spring of our married life was upon us. We had started our family and felt optimistic about the prospect of everything that spring would bring. Our happy baby is a joy and I am determined I will be the best farmer's wife I can be and I do my part to make farming a success.

My plan was to raise chickens to give us a bountiful supply of meat for meals and eggs to sell to avoid charging groceries. At this time we still had no money. The gain from the previous year's crops went to pay off debts. So, I thought, why not raise turkeys, geese and ducks as well? I had no idea how much work I was taking on.

The tom and two hen turkeys produced 93 poults at the local hatchery and they got off to a good start, as did the ducks and geese. In the meantime the chicks feathered out and we could hardly wait for the dinners we'd be enjoying with fried chicken piled high on platters and served with new potatoes, creamed peas and other fresh produce. I was excited at the thought, but really didn't have a clue about what I was in for. I suppose I assumed that all that poultry was just going to strut around the big barnyard and with no effort at all grow up, get fat and be healthy. In my imaginings we would feast on roast duck and spring chicken dinners and then sell enough turkeys at Thanksgiving to go on a shopping spree for Christmas gifts for my entire family. However, as I "counted my chickens" my dreams came to a sudden halt.

We often spent Saturday evenings at my folks' place in St Marys. We'd overnight there and attend early Mass so we could return home in time for the morning chores. One

Sunday, the first thing we noticed was that our big German Shepherd, Hans, was nowhere to be seen. We called. No answer, no big bouncing, tail-wagging, face-licking welcome. Something was wrong.

As we approached the coop to feed the hungry birds, our hearts sank. The door hung open. The coup was empty. Where were the chickens? Big truck tire marks in the yard told the story. We'd been robbed. There were just a few chickens left, hardly enough to provide eggs through the next winter. And still no Hans. Johnny was heartsick: they'd stolen our dog too.

Two days later I was pumping water from our well when out of the cornfield that bordered the yard came our dear Hans, crawling on his belly. I ran to him. He could hardly lift his head to greet me with his wet kisses. On his chest was dried blood around a puncture wound. They had shot him. How he managed to crawl off into the cornfield and survive for three days was a miracle. After taking care of his thirst and helping him to the porch, I impatiently awaited Johnny's return from the fields to share the good news.

Over the next weeks, we fed Hans and watered him and nursed him back to health. We knew he had been a hero trying to protect the chicks in his charge. Fortunately, on the night of the attack he managed to vanish into the darkness and hide in the field. Surely, that is what saved his life. In the meantime, the thieves made off with the chickens—and my hopes of contributing a bit to our prosperity.

Later, Johnny told me that he suspected that our magnificent German Shepherd had been shot in retaliation for Johnny's refusal to pay into a "protection" scam foisted on farmers by a corrupt Kansas City political machine. I think he didn't tell me at the time because he didn't want to scare me.

After the chicken debacle, I put all my efforts into producing the turkeys. We were pleased that the 93 poults continued to do well. It was a well-known fact that any "amateur" attempt to raise turkeys was an effort in futility. A turkey dinner on

Our farm at Sandy Hook.

Thanksgiving Day was not a given. Most farmers had a flock of geese or ducks to supply the special holiday meal as a back up. Our flock seemed to be thriving and our hopes were high for success. We thought we were doing things right, but we didn't know about the lethal damage the pernicious weed cocklebur would do the flock. Cocklebur grew along the fence of the enclosed field where they spent their days. We lost about a third of them before we discovered the problem. The remaining flock flourished for a while until they developed an infection and we lost more of them. Finally, when we had a couple dozen beautiful, growing turkeys, a coyote attack put our poultry growing efforts to rest for good.

And I haven't even told the story of the ducks!

My disaster with the poultry left this young farmer's wife utterly discouraged about trying to improve our situation. I also felt firsthand the hopelessness that farmers must experience when their crops fail despite enormous investments of labor and resources. Johnny, through no fault of his own, sustained crop losses for four years. He'd rented land on a small island in the Kaw River when he started farming on his own. His first season produced a good crop of corn, but it only paid him five cents a bushel so there was no income that year. The best he could do with the corn was to burn it in the heating stove that winter to keep warm. The next year floods destroyed the entire crop. This was followed by the 1934 drought and dust storms. In 1935 he moved to Sandy Hook and suffered another Kaw River flood. His fields turned into a soggy jumble of ragged corn stocks, salvaged only for feeding livestock.

The very first sentence our little son ever uttered gave me pause. He was walking and just beginning to talk when one day he looked up at the sky and said, "Tink gonna wain?"

"Oh my God! The life of a farmer," I thought. It was too much to bear.

"Yes, my dear little son, I think it is going to rain and rain and fill the river bed until it overflows into the fields and leaves the promise of a good crop in a muddy, rotten mess. Or maybe it won't rain at all, and the wind will blow hot until everything dries up. Haven't we seen it all?"

But hope springs eternal and God is good. I was cheered that spring of 1938 because the wheat fields were beautiful and green. There had been plenty of rain and just the right amount of sun. The corn was planted and long rows of young stocks were showing off like soldiers on the march.

"Surely, this year there will be a good crop," I dared to hope.

The Combine

The good news for 1938 was that we had a bountiful wheat crop and Johnny bought a combine. A combine was a newly developed machine that would reap and thresh in one operation. It would clip the tops off the stalk, and then separate the grain from stalks and husks so the grain alone could be loaded onto a truck. It required only two people to harvest a wheat field, eliminating the need for a threshing crew—and abruptly breaking down a long-honored tradition. No more shoveling by hand, a back-breaking job. No more cooking for the threshers.

So, guess who was driving the truck? Me! We had purchased two used Model T trucks. I would back one up to the combine and wait for the grain to pour down until the truck was full. Then I would drive the truck to the elevator in St. Marys, the nearest town, to deliver the grain. Once it was deposited at the elevator I'd drive back to the field and pick up the second truck which was filled by then and return to the elevator in St. Marys. These trips would continue until the end of the day or the field was clean, whichever came first.

Johnny told me to collect the money for the grain and take it directly to the bank so we could pay our bills. The money we received paid all the debts for the previous year. I was proud of the way I had helped with the harvest that year.

However, unbeknownst to our neighbors we were secretly planning to do something unusual for farmers.

The Plan

During the summer of 1938 Johnny and I made a decision. We resolved to leave the farm and build a new life in the city. Johnny saw no future in renting. He had enough experience to know how uncertain farming could be. He also saw all the young folks from the surrounding farming community go off to the city to find work. We wondered about the family we hoped to have and if that would be the pattern with our children. One night as we were discussing our possible future we decided it would be all right to move to the city. We could make a home for our family there and have better schools. Deciding *where* to move was also a serious decision, but for us an easy one.

Johnny's uncle, "Doc" Kramer, had a successful dental practice in Aberdeen, Washington, so Johnny had heard a lot about the beauty of the Northwest and its mild climate. There it was. If we were leaving Kansas, Washington it would be! Most people moved to California if they had the urge to move, but that was not for us. My husband had great dreams of fishing for salmon, deer hunting in the mountains and enjoying all the great outdoors sports that he read about in his "Field and Stream" magazine. So Washington it was—and I was ready to move.

We took our parenting very seriously and figured on more children. Johnny, an only son whose father died when he was nine months old, looked forward to having a big family, but it scared me a little to think of raising a family in the city. I discussed this with my pastor who grew up on the tough side of Chicago. He assured me we would be fine. "My child," he said, "you will meet many saints in the city."

We continued planting and harvesting for another two years. During the last year we put our plan into action by planting wheat hoping to harvest it the following summer. It was the custom for farmers who rent the land and plan to move to plant a crop for the next year. We followed the custom, then gave notice to the landlord that we would be leaving after the harvest in early July.

To make our dream a reality we needed to have a farm sale. We advertised the sale for the last week in February, 1940. A large crowd of farm neighbors came to look over our sale items. The combine, of which we were so proud and that had saved us so much work, was the first to sell. The rest of the equipment down to the last rake and milking stool also disappeared from the yard. With our sale and now three good years of crops, we were finally debt free and had what seemed a substantial amount of money to start our new adventure. We had even paid off the loan that Johnny had taken out to buy his first team of mules six years earlier.

Now that we had sold all our belongings it was time to tell our neighbors and other friends our secret plans. Of course, there were a great many questions during our farm sale, but we were firm in our determination to move to Seattle to start our new life. We now had two children, Jack, age two, and Margie, six months old.

Fear and Guilt

During this stressful year of preparing to leave our families and move far away, I began to have panic attacks. I was utterly terrorized with fear, not of our move, but of the growing threat of war. The very names of Joseph Stalin or Adolph Hitler caused me distress, and the prophecies that were surfacing in religious circles about the end of the world only intensified my panic. I didn't want Johnny to know what was causing my loss of sleep, appetite and weight. I realize now that I probably also had postpartum depression after Margie's birth. I was a basket case but I couldn't talk about it.

I also carried a guilt trip that was completely unreasonable. It would come and go over and over. No one could know the suffering. I prayed for deliverance and I thought the move away would solve the problem. My father had died at the age of 58 earlier that year, 1939, and I grieved at the thought of leaving my mother, who was in frail health. She had no income and had to depend on her children to maintain the home.

My brother Archie was now seventeen and still so completely helpless there was not much choice but to take him to a state facility for care. Johnny and I drove the 200 mile trip to Winfield, Kansas with my sister Rita. I was six or seven months pregnant at the time. My mother was unable to make the trip.

It was very sad to leave Archie among strangers. I did not feel reassured that anyone there would love him or treat him with a caring heart. One of the sorrows of my life is that we didn't realize that cerebral palsy doesn't necessarily affect the intelligence or emotions. Since Archie never learned to talk I suppose we underestimated his intellect, and because I had to leave home to work for other people I wasn't able to be with him very much after that. If there is anything I could redo in my life, it would be to create a better life for him. Archie lived to age 35. He died in 1957.

As for my depression it came and went. In the meantime, I threw myself into a very busy life on the farm and the plans for our great adventure scheduled for July 1940.

The day before we left for the West in early July, 1940, we went to St. Benedict's Abby in Atchison to say good-bye to Brother Paul. Here we are with Jack, 2 ½ and Margie, 8 months old.

Most of my brothers and sisters joined us on the visit. Pictured here are Dick, Oscar, Fred, Leo, myself, Johnny, Otto (with his bride, Elizabeth McDermott), Rita and Paul. Jack and Buddy are in front.

CHAPTER SIX
THE MOVE WEST

To Seattle and Back

Amazingly, everything went along as scheduled prior to our departure from Kansas. Johnny had finished a course at the trade school in Kansas City, the wheat crop was harvested, the debts were paid off and we were ready for our big trip. We planned to visit Johnny's favorite cousins in Los Angeles, see the Grand Canyon and other tourist destinations on the way.

We left Kansas in our 1936 Ford just after the Fourth of July, 1940. The first day we drove via US 40 as far as Colorado

Here we are in Los Angeles visiting Johnny's Kramer cousins.

Springs. Johnny wanted to see Pike's Peak. Next we made our way south to Santa Fe, a completely different world from the one we knew. At Flagstaff, Arizona, we rested during the day so we could make the journey through the desert that night. Arriving at Needles, California the next morning, weary and hot, we were only 260 miles from Los Angeles.

Johnny's relatives welcomed us to a needed respite after our tiring journey. Fortunately for us, most of his cousins were on vacation so they had time to dedicate to their out-of-town visitors. They took us on typical sightseeing tours to show off the marvels of their adopted state and we had a wonderful two weeks there. We saw the ocean for the first time and visited Hollywood. They tried to convince us to remain in California since they were all doing well in Los Angeles—one cousin worked at Douglass Aircraft, one was a professor at Loyola University, and another was a nurse. It was all exciting, but California wasn't a serious option for us. We, who wanted to raise our kids in the city, found *that* city entirely too fast. So, while we appreciated their hospitality, on we went up the coast toward our original destination, arriving in Seattle on a bright day in early August 1940.

We knew exactly two people in the area. They were the brothers of my new sister-in-law, Elizabeth. She was a "McDermott," a member of a large Irish Catholic family in St. Marys. When she married my brother Otto the year before, we learned that her brothers John and Joe were doing part of their medical training at Providence Hospital, Seattle. It was comforting to know there were folks from "back home" in our new, but unfamiliar, city.

At first, we rented a cabin near Tukwila about fifteen miles from Seattle while we looked for a more permanent place to live. To get our bearings, we were eager to see our new city and had identified several sites and attractions we wanted to take in. Our list included Seattle's waterfront, the Pike Place Public Market, the Smith Tower (the "tallest building West of the Mississippi" so we were told), the recently constructed

Grandma Schuler visits us in Seattle in late 1941. Jim is the baby.

Floating Bridge across Lake Washington that had just opened in June, and other Seattle landmarks. We needed to be tourists a bit longer before we could settle down. So there we were on Pike Street in downtown Seattle heading toward Alaska Way and who do we see crossing the street? It is Joe McDermott from St. Marys! It is a good sign. Of the nearly 400,000 people living in Seattle at the time who might have been crossing that street at that moment, we see someone from our home town in Kansas. We are off to a good start.

In our search for more permanent housing we found a partially built home for sale in Burien. Johnny got a job at a Chevrolet agency and for the first time ever we had a weekly paycheck to count on. Johnny spent days at his job; in the evenings and on weekends he worked at finishing the house. By then, I was expecting our third child. Jim was born the following July.

During that period we had regular contact with the McDermotts, and through the years followed their careers as John and Joe developed into prominent members of the medical profession in Seattle. Joe later became our family doctor, but first and foremost he was a friend, a kind and generous person, much loved by our kids. Joe did house calls when no one else was doing them. His untimely death in his early forties left a void in our hearts.

Within a few years three of my brothers, Leo, Dick and Fred, moved to Seattle looking for work and made it their home. My sister Agnes came out to the Northwest with her husband who was from Port Angeles, a town on the Olympic peninsula. Eventually, there were more than a few family and friends from St. Marys in the area and the Seattle-St. Marys connection we appreciated so much on our arrival in 1940 only deepened over time.

Marge, Jim and Jack, in Seattle, 1941.

One thing we hadn't anticipated before we came to Seattle was the rapid escalation of the war in Europe. We'd made the decision to leave the farm in 1938 and held our farm sale in early 1940. By the time we arrived in Seattle, the news from Europe was full of foreboding. I began again to suffer from anxiety over what was to become of our future. Jim was not yet five months old when the Japanese attacked Pearl Harbor. It was a terrifying time. Seattle wasn't yet "home," and taking care of three small children far from family with no close friends nearby took its toll. The draft went into immediate effect, and we unexpectedly had to reevaluate our move. We feared that if Johnny were suddenly called to military service I'd be left alone in Seattle with the kids, almost two thousand miles from my family. Reluctantly, we made the decision to return to Kansas. Expecting to farm once again, we made the trip in May, 1942, with three kids and a puppy.

Yet, after all the inconvenience of moving again, our sojourn back in St Marys turned out to be short. After a few months, a change in army policy reassured us that Johnny, who was 36 at that point, would not be drafted. Farming was not proving as successful as we had hoped, and the experience of living once again in a small town reinvigorated our desire for urban living and reminded us why we had left in the first place.

There was plenty of land for rent but there were no farm implements to be had. So Johnny got a defense job, commuting to Topeka from St. Marys to help build Forbes Air Base. After that job he worked on a similar one in Salina, which was too far to commute. He had to get a room there while I lived in a rented house next to his mother, Maggie Schuler, in St. Marys. Up to that point we had lived in the country in a little farm-house in a timber of oak trees being cut down and sold for making rifle butts. It was a lonesome time. I was once again pregnant, this time with our fourth child, and as usual suffering from morning sickness. So I was glad to move into town to a house with plumbing. But every day I had to make the trip back to the country to check on the animals that we'd bought

On our return to Seattle, in 1943 we had four children:
Margie, Jack, Jim and Vince, the baby.

in anticipation of farming, including a dozen pigs, some sheep, and a steer calf to fatten.

Vince was born on February 27, 1943. Johnny had finally gotten released from the defense job and was working in a local garage on commission—a truly non-profit arrangement! One day he came home with a pittance of a check and it helped us make another decision. Vince was four or five months old and war in Europe was raging. Hitler was stomping all over Europe and there were reports of attacks on ships on the East Coast. Despite all that, we decided we'd had enough of Kansas and not enough of Washington. We knew Johnny would have no trouble getting work.

Return to Seattle—For Good

This time around we were very broke, our tires were not good and we'd have to transport our refrigerator, washing machine and a couple of other irreplaceable items in a two wheel trailer. But for another chance for us to dwell in that gorgeous scenery we would make every effort to integrate ourselves into that chosen land. The climate was mild, the rains gentle, no blizzards or tornadoes. To us the sight of Mt. Rainier at sunset was awe-inspiring, and a winter glimpse of the snow covered Olympic Mountains above the blue waters of Puget Sound was definitely a scenic block-buster. We wanted more.

It was a long, hard, incredibly hot, wretched journey that included flat tires, camping in a tent, and a broken axle on the trailer in Laramie, Wyoming, where we unexpectedly had to stay several days waiting for parts to be delivered. To add insult to injury, I got a case of shingles along the way. For me misery is traveling in a car without air conditioning with four little kids—one still an infant—in the heat and dust of August with painful blisters over my shoulders and back. Eventually, we made it to Cle Elum, Washington, where I went to a doctor and got relief.

While there we heard how impossible it was to get housing in Seattle, with the influx of so many people looking for "defense work." We decided I would remain with the kids in North Bend, about 40 miles east of Seattle, while Johnny went to town to seek employment and find us a place to live. A few days later he came back to get us. No matter how hard it was, I continually thanked God that unlike thousands of young wives and mothers who were struggling without their husbands, mine was at my side, not on a far away battlefield. At that point in our national defense policy neither age nor the number of dependents deferred a healthy man from military service, only defense work. So we still faced that vague possibility that Johnny would have to go to war, though I trusted that he would never have to.

Integrating back into Seattle was not easy. Who wants to rent to a couple with four little kids? The choices were grim. We wound up renting two rooms in the south end of Seattle in the most awful gray complex of attached cabins. Centrally located public toilets served all 40 units. It looked and felt like an internment camp.

Johnny started back to work at a Chevrolet dealership as a car body repairman. His skill was in demand as it was important to keep all vehicles in working order. There were no new cars being manufactured, only tanks and they were not for sale to the general public.

Soon after we got settled in and Johnny had worked a couple of weeks, a co-worker wanted him to go on a deer hunting trip with him. With meat being so scarce the thought of venison steaks and roasts was tempting. Also, getting a deer was an unfulfilled dream for Johnny who loved to hunt, but in Kansas it was mostly for rabbits. So they agreed: if anyone got a deer, it would be split equally. And, yes, they did get a deer. Freezer lockers had just been invented. They rented one close to the other hunter and far from us and by the time we finally went to the locker, there was nothing there but some soup bones!

While Johnny was gone on that hunting trip the kids came down with chicken pox. Baby Vince was so covered you couldn't have put a pin head between the pox. It was an unusually severe outbreak. Later we learned they probably got the virus from my shingles. Shortly after they recovered from the pox, I discovered I was expecting our fifth child.

By then, we found another place to live, still far from town, miserable and inadequate, but at least a house, unattached to anything with a lot of space out of doors for the kids to play. A dense evergreen forest bordered the property and we felt quite isolated there. The greatest entertainment for the kids was to watch the formations of B 19 Bombers flying over, preparing to go overseas. The children had few toys, but Jack and Jim would take clothespins, connect them and pretend they were airplanes.

Johnny would leave for work before six in the morning and not return until nine or ten at night, which meant that I and my four little ones were alone during long, lonely winter days in a bleak house with no electricity. It took a while for me to learn how to work with the damp fir logs I piled in the pot-bellied stove to heat the house. As surely as I got a decent fire going it would go out, leaving the kids shivering and me trying again frantically to discover the secret of building a fire with damp wood. Of course, I caught the worst cold of my life.

We knew we couldn't continue in that situation and needed to get serious about finding a home, but we were hindered in many ways by the big "war effort" of 1944. Gasoline was rationed as was butter, coffee and several other essentials, and there was very little film to keep the memory of my darling babies. Daddy worked long hours during the week and tried to make up for lost time on the week-ends. So with the lack of time and gasoline to do the needed exploring and get our bearings, it took a while to get settled. We wanted to locate near a Catholic school, for Jack was now nearing six, having missed out on kindergarten. I was in my sixth month of pregnancy with Carol and still had no doctor lined up. The few doctors who weren't in the service didn't want any new patients. We worried about who would take care of me. We just had to trust the Good Lord and we prayed a lot.

Woodlawn and St Benedict's

I don't know by what miracle we found St. Benedict School in the north end of Seattle. Maybe we took the kids to see Woodland Park Zoo and accidentally stumbled across that school building four blocks from the park. Or maybe we set out that day with a deliberate plan to explore the Wallingford and Green Lake neighborhoods. But however we got there, when we saw that two-story brick building with birch lime-stone trim and the name, "St. Benedict School," engraved in

St. Benedict's parish school. For the first few years we were here, the school auditorium also served as our church.

stone above the door, it felt both familiar and comforting. We knew we were nearing the end of our journey.

The real estate agent we contacted that very day found us a two bedroom home a mile from the school on Woodlawn Avenue. It had a small but lovely view of Green Lake, a white picket fence, and a price tag of only $3,950. Green Lake, the jewel of Seattle's north end, was only 100 paces from our door. The home and neighborhood looked wonderful to us after nearly four years of the very difficult housing situations we had endured. We accomplished the transaction by redeeming our small cache of savings bonds and borrowing the balance of the down payment from my brother, Dick, who had moved to Seattle with our brother, Leo, two years earlier. Dick had a job at Boeing.

We purchased two sets of bunk beds for the kids. At long last our bedroom furniture arrived by train and we bought a hide-a-bed for additional sleeping. We moved in on February 5, 1944. It was almost civilization. We'd made the decision to leave the farm and move to the city six years earlier. It had been a long journey, but the pieces were beginning to fall into place. We were finally in the "city."

Our little house on Woodlawn.

Carol Jean was born four months later on June 8, 1944, at a most critical point in World War II. The invasion by our troops into mainland Europe had begun in earnest that very week. The first attempt to land at Dunquerque, France months earlier was a total disaster. The Germans were waiting for them. It was another of the many tragic events and battles lost, but then things got more hopeful. "D Day" had arrived after long months of waiting. Thousands of troops assembled and waited in England for the day when they could cross the English Channel and storm overland to stop Hitler, the "madman." Japan had aligned with Germany and Italy to form the Axis and the battles would go on. All of this was happening at the time of Carol's birth and my five-day stay in the hospital.

"Saints in the City"

My dear mother made the trip out to Seattle from Topeka by bus in early June, her very first out-of-state trip. Dick's wife, Lorraine, and I were both expecting, and we both had little girls a week apart. So Mom was our heroine.

Johnny and I hadn't gotten acquainted with anyone in our parish up to then. We were busy trying to make a home and integrate into the neighborhood. My dream of finally living in a real neighborhood in the city came with its own challenges. From my perspective, Seattle was a decidedly non-Catholic city. I heard somewhere that it was still considered "mission territory." As happy as I was to be here, and even though I knew life in the city would be different, much of it felt alien to me. I missed the morning, noon and evening Angeles bells and wished that some of the people in our new neighborhood had been Catholic. The Greek Orthodox family next door was friendlier than the Pentecostals on the other side, but most had little sympathy for the new young family with four little children and one on the way. Subtle expressions of narrow-mindedness—"Oh, you're *Catholic!*"—made it difficult not to be a bit defensive. I didn't appreciate the Woodlawn debate over the size of our family.

My mom made the trip to Seattle again two years later when I was about to give birth to Larry, our sixth child. Being a very sociable person, Mom couldn't understand why we still had not made friends. Neither Johnny nor I were very outgoing, in fact, we were both rather shy. To have friends, a support group and a social life was not even a dream at this time in our lives. Johnny worked long hours during the week. Saturdays were always busy catching up on chores, and Sundays were taken up with church and usually long drives when gas became available. It was a very lonesome time. During Mass I'd look around and see many other couples with children who all seemed to be acquainted with each other. I remember thinking back to our dear old pastor's advice on our choice of moving from the farm to the city. He said to me, "My child, you will meet many saints in the city and you can become a saint in the city." I was beginning to wonder where they were. I asked God this question because I hadn't met anyone—good, bad or indifferent. But I trusted and hoped that someday we'd have friends.

My mother was pretty upset with us about this. One Sunday she heard an announcement at church that there would be a Mothers Club picnic and informed me that we were going.

The family on the day of Jack's First Communion. Marge, Vince, Jim and Jack are in the front. Carol is the baby.

She helped me get the six kids ready, made an attempt at packing a picnic and headed to Woodland Park. We ended up at table six. And we did meet other women there. You couldn't have been with my mother and not meet people. She advised me: "You can't just meet people halfway; you have to go beyond the halfway mark. You must reach out to them!" That was really good advice; it helped me overcome my shyness and I soon discovered others had the same problem.

Soon after that it was time for Jack to join the Cub Scouts and my prayers were answered. Suddenly, we had more friends than we could handle. We were invited to join a pinochle club with five other couples. And wonder of wonders, I was hearing people say "How marvelous," and other encouraging things when they learned I was expecting my seventh child.

A surprise baby shower (my first) brought me a pretty bassinet filled with lovely gifts. I'm sure my new friends never realized how much their gesture meant to me. I was not only grateful, but filled with a sense of self worth. And when it came time for delivery, we had many offers of help.

Johnny was also invited to join a poker club with men active in scouting. They all loved to fish and hunt. In fact they named their group "The Fish Buyers Club," because one time they had taken two boats out to salmon fish, challenging each other to bring in the most fish. It was a totally negative fishing trip—not a nibble for either group. But they each spotted locals on the beach with big catches and separately bought several "beauties." Arriving back at the boat house for the big weigh in, they discovered that both boat loads of fishing buddies had done the same thing. The hilarity of that discovery became legendary and they never tired of its retelling.

On the day of Rose Mary's birth, June 24, 1947, Johnny's union went on strike. His shop closed and the strike went on until Christmas Eve. Fortunately for us, Johnny was able to find work in a shop outside Seattle unaffected by the strike. He had to take the Leschi ferry from Madison Park, Seattle to Kirkland. It was a small ferry and sometimes very frightening when it was stormy on Lake Washington. He went back to Davies Chevrolet after the strike was settled and eventually hired in at Callahan's Auto Rebuild where he stayed until his retirement in December, 1980.

CHAPTER SEVEN

WALLINGFORD

A Very Special House

By 1947 the housing situation was getting serious again. Jack, Marge and Jim were in St Benedict's School and Vince, Carol, Larry and Rose Mary were preschoolers. Housing prices had inflated as our needs escalated, and with all those strikes, Johnny's income was still not adequate. We were afraid of taking on a bigger house. Every time the subject came up, I was more discouraged. If ever I needed a miracle, it was then.

We'd definitely outgrown the starter house bought in 1944, but we had not begun a search as yet. One day a realtor looking for a listing rang our doorbell. I nearly grabbed him by the necktie. That very evening he took us to a beautiful, spacious house which we agreed to buy. But the inspection revealed some problems which required a lot of updating before we could get an FHA loan. That deal fell through, but we were finally off in search of an adequate house.

We were shown many "fixer-uppers," none of which answered our needs. Our top priority, next to "living space," was to be within walking distance of St. Benedict's School and Church. We had dreams about the home we would make for our children in our chosen city. We were seriously praying to St. Therese who promised to spend her heaven "doing good on earth." But after six months of searching and praying, there was still no house.

One day on my walk to St Benedict's, I noticed a house that reminded me of "the home place" where my dad grew up. It had a front porch with pillars and a wisteria vine, but there was no indication it was for sale. A while later some acquaintances who lived on Wallingford Avenue invited us to pick cherries from a tree in their yard. Johnny came home with a basket of sweet cherries and excitement over a home he had viewed from the top of a tall ladder.

"This place has a yard at least 200 feet deep, a dozen fruit trees—apples, pears, plums, cherry, crabapple—and a grape arbor. There'd be lots of space for the kids to play and the house looks big enough."

Imagine my delight when I realized it was the same house I had seen from the front. I didn't even know it had a back yard. We were so drawn to this place that we felt we needed to make an extra effort. Getting up our courage we rang the doorbell and asked the lady who answered, "Will this house possibly be for sale any time soon?" To our surprise, she said, "Yes. My mother just passed away and we are planning to sell it." She showed us the interior and we knew this was the house we were looking for. On the spot we made a verbal agreement on the purchase price, $8,000.

A week later she changed her mind. She didn't know we had "all those kids."

Meanwhile, the realtor came by to show us one more house and I was in tears. I told him the story and, incredibly, he knew the house and the owner, Mrs. Andersen. He went to see her and came back an hour later with the good news. He convinced her that no one but a big family would buy it because of all the updating needed, and he got her to agree to a $7,000 sale price and include the furniture as well.

Now it was urgent that we sell the house on Woodlawn. Going into winter things were slow, the days short and the market sluggish. There were all kinds of obstacles, but we managed to close a deal. Our equity made a good down payment on our beautiful new house.

We moved in on February 24, 1948. It had been a mild winter, there were still roses blooming in the front flower beds. The bushes had been pruned and the roses tossed on the lawn. I remembered St. Therese's promise. "I will send down from heaven a shower of roses." Maybe they were a little withered, but there were still buds unopened. I was convinced St. Therese had heard our prayers.

That moving day in 1948 started simply as a matter of loading up what the family possessed and transferring it to the new house. Johnny and some generous friends moved beds and cribs and lamps and boxes of clothing and utensils into our new place. But something else, something extraordinary, happened that day.

Mrs. Andersen had included in the sale several pieces of furniture that had been in the house from its beginning. She left a couple of maple beds, chests and tables, and a mirrored oak hall chair, but the most astonishing thing Mrs. Andersen left was an oil painting of Mount Rainier. It was a painting so exquisite that it could change its mood throughout the day as the light filtered into the living room from the east, strong and forceful at sunrise, and soft and subdued at dusk as the haze

The house in 1948.

in the valley settled into the night. That image of Mount Rainier would become a most treasured feature of our home, but on moving day, the day it came into our lives, it gave us something very special. The painting touched our souls and we knew somehow that we had acquired the very spirit of our new home.

That evening I fixed supper on the wood-burning cook stove that had served as the home's kitchen range for the past 40 years. Of course, that stove would soon be replaced with an electric one, but what a joy it was to prepare and share the first meal on Wallingford. Everything was big and new and exciting to the kids as they explored their new house. It had a front hall, a living room with sliding doors, bay windows, and a dining room with a dish rail! After supper when all the beds had been assembled and it was time to settle in for the night, we all went *upstairs* to bed.

It did not take long for all of us to feel that this was truly "home." We'd gone from a cabin in the woods to a small house on Woodlawn to a new larger home on Wallingford—and we knew this was where we belonged, that we had found a place in our promised land. It became the home that would witness

The house today.

82

the triumphs and defeats, the struggles and successes of all the Schuler kids who would grow up there. The seven who arrived that day and five yet to be born would be linked forever to 5515 Wallingford. The house itself would undergo many changes—a ceiling replaced here or bathroom added there were to be expected—but there were also the experiments our enterprising kids undertook, like the intercom system one of the boys installed throughout the whole house or the permanent model train display in the basement surrounded by wall murals hand painted by our artistic children. On the grounds trees would grow, fruit, die and be replaced and Johnny's fuchsias and begonias would eventually give way to my roses and clematis. For decades, 5515 Wallingford would be synonymous with the Schulers.

The Garden Grows

The first year in our home on Wallingford Avenue was exciting as we discovered the bounty that was blossoming in our own back yard. The trees fruited with sweet cherries, crabapples, pears, apples and Italian prunes. In the far corner were rows of blackberries and raspberries. There was space for a vegetable garden and closer to the house was a grape arbor. Oh, we were busy canning and preserving as the summer progressed. Plums and pears, apple sauce, blackberry jam and raspberry jelly were all ready for storage in the basement. In our garden several rows of prolific "Kentucky Wonder" green beans inspired us to buy a big pressure cooker. That first year we canned two hundred quarts of green beans. But we soon discovered that the carrots, turnips and radishes were worm riddled. I didn't want to use the newly marketed pesticides being pushed at the time. So we stuck with lettuce, cabbage and green beans. Summer salads came right from the garden to the table. Like the farm in Kansas, our city "farm" on Wallingford gave us food we could preserve and count on for our winter meals. And as part of our summer fun, we always made a trip in June or July to "pick-your-own" strawberry and raspberry fields on the islands of Puget Sound, augmenting our larder even more. The tomatoes, apricots and peaches came in flats from the sunny side of Washington—from Yakima. Such bounty! We were happy to be here.

Our property on Wallingford was unique in that we had five lots bordering ours on the south, two on the west and one to the north. That meant we had eight neighbor families observing every activity in our yard. There was definitely a need for privacy. Since the original fences around the perimeter were collapsing with age and needed to be removed, we decided to replace them with a laurel hedge. One hundred plants and a few years later our back yard became a private park with an impenetrable broad-leafed evergreen fence that grew to great heights with ease.

One of our special joys was having enough space to create both play space and a flower garden. In addition to the

The lower lawn in spring covered with pink cherry blossoms.

obligatory sand box, Johnny built a swing set with monkey bar, slide and seesaw, strong enough to outlast every single Schuler child and then some. Before a deck was added to the house, the space under the grape arbor served as special shaded patio for outdoor eating and summer relaxation.

The reality of the flower garden began on a slope south of the house with a few hanging baskets, a big flower box filled with petunias, and a couple of rhododendron bushes. As time went on we were discovering numerous types of flowers that thrive in the mild Pacific Northwest climate we had never seen in Kansas. There were primroses, fuchsias, begonias and many other plants we couldn't name but knew we wanted. We also wanted to have a shrine to the Blessed Mother.

Little by little our plan became a reality. In August, 1952, we used our two-week vacation to build a grotto and dig a pond. From our exploratory travels we'd discovered a gorgeous

"5515"

85

creek fifteen miles northeast of Seattle full of beautiful river rock. Our vacation that year included several "pilgrimage" trips to the creek to gather the rocks and pebbles we needed for our garden. By the end we'd built a pond with a bridge, an island and a lighthouse, as well as a grotto, a bird bath, a fountain, some pedestals and a wishing well—all made of concrete and meant to last for years. The construction phase, the hard part of creating our future flower garden, was now over. Next came the arrangement of the beds and borders as we tried to visualize what spring might generate. The garden got fenced, of course, because ponds and children don't mix.

A statue for the grotto was a top priority but we were still on a limited budget and had to plan carefully. Johnny found one at the St Vincent de Paul Salvage Bureau but it was not for sale. Fortunately, our friend, Charlie Albert, who was instrumental in establishing the first St Vincent de Paul Society chapter in Seattle, came to our rescue. "Yes," he told us, "the statue has a 'sold' sign on it. Pick it up on your way home from work." So Mary became part of our garden and over the years helped me watch over all the children who came to our play yard.

That first year we managed to plant some tulip and daffodil bulbs to give us a jump start in the spring. That was just the

The pond and grotto.

beginning. Friends donated plants and Johnny, ever the farmer, learned to start fuchsias. For many years in late winter he could be found in his garden shed under the house after work getting his plants rooted in a special mixture of vermiculite and Vigoro.

After a few years we had many hanging baskets of fuchsias with dozens of varieties and combinations of red, pink, white and purple. The tuberous begonias came in brilliant colors across the spectrum. These "new" flowers, along with the "older" roses, lilacs, peonies, rhododendrons and other shrubs and perennials made our garden a spectacular sight. It turned out to be almost a tourist attraction as friends consistently brought their out-of-town visitors to see it.

For Johnny and me our garden was a source of great pride and gratitude.

The Children of 5515

The year after we moved into our new home we were expecting the next addition to our family, our eighth child. We looked forward to a baby girl, hoping we could settle for four boys and four girls. But God had other plans for us. David arrived on February 11, 1949.

Baby David was nearly three when our Joan Marie made her appearance on March 14, 1952. I was so happy to have a baby girl to enjoy the years ahead, thinking of course, that she would be the last addition to our family. Yet again, God had other plans for us.

Greg was born August 7, 1955. Joan adored her little brother and as soon as possible she had him dancing with her to the ballet music on our new stereo. When Greg was four, Joseph, our seventh son, was born on July 10, 1959—coincidentally, the feast of the "Seven Holy Brothers."

Soon after he was born, doctors discovered that Joe had a complication that required a blood exchange. Until then I was unaware that I had the Rh negative blood factor. It had not been an issue with my first ten babies. It probably had something to do with the transfusions I had received two years earlier. Babies born with this complication often did not make it, but our baby thrived on his new blood and was a healthy, happy child.

God still had plans for us. There was to be one more baby. Because of the Rh issue, I was carefully monitored during my pregnancy. A medication being developed for mothers and babies with this problem was not yet available and I was told to expect the worst when each blood test revealed an increase in antibodies. Happily, our baby, Paul, was born alive, but, like Joe, he needed to be rushed to Children's Hospital for a complete blood exchange. Thanks to the marvels of modern medicine, he passed the crisis and came home to us several days later.

Paul's birth was on December 10, 1961. During Christmas week, Archbishop Thomas J. Connolly, as was his custom, came to our parish church for the formal ceremony of infant baptism for a twelfth child. Even though Paul had been baptized right after birth in the hospital, we were honored by the Archbishop's gesture.

With baby Joan, 1952.

Vince with Happy, another family member, 1949.

The "middle" family having a good laugh. David and Larry in the back. In front, Rose Mary holding Greg, and Joan, 1956.

My boys: Above, Jack Jim, Vince, Larry, David and
Greg. Below, Joe, holding baby Paul, 1962,

The Schuler Family at St. Benedict School
1944 through 1976

Jack   Margaret   Jim   Vince

Carol Jean   Larry   Rose Mary   David

Joan   Greg   Joseph   Paul

My girls: Marge, Carol, Rose Mary and Joan.

One month after Paul's baptism, on January 20, 1962, Johnny and I celebrated our silver wedding anniversary, and we had a lot to celebrate. We'd had twelve beautiful, healthy children. We were grateful for our home, our neighborhood, our parish and school, and our community of friends in Seattle. We hoped that we were cooperating with God's plan that was unfolding in our lives and gave thanks for all we were receiving.

CHAPTER EIGHT

A PATCHWORK QUILT OF MEMORIES

Over the Years

All of the stories that can and maybe should be told about my life on Wallingford as a parent, wife and friend are too numerous to recount. I know that the experiences of my growing up years, good or bad, had an influence on my perspective on life and especially on my parenting. I also know that once you become a parent, it is a full time, ongoing, amateur effort, full of blunders and successes, with the saving grace of a lot of love poured out and received.

Here, I offer a patchwork quilt of memories, a series of vignettes, that comprise but a sample of the many chapters that could be written about the joys, sorrows, adventures, struggles and accomplishments in my process of living over the past many years.

Making Ends Meet

Raising twelve kids on a single paycheck was a challenge, but I was determined that we would do it and never have a bill collector at our door.

Learning to manage our finances when we moved to the city, however, took some adjustment. My husband was born into a farm culture. As a young boy he lived in the country on a farm with his widowed mother, his grandparents, two single uncles, and a single aunt. Farmers' income was seasonal. When the crops came in they paid their bills. Working with a monthly budget routine was not part of the farm experience. In addition, in that culture the husband was the provider and the wife was not to worry about money or bills.

When we left the farm and moved to the city, Johnny found employment and a steady paycheck. All well and good, but the farm mentality lingered. Paying bills on a monthly schedule didn't seem that important and it didn't occur to Johnny that I could play a role.

Time for a decision! Someone has to pay the bills, and it was plain to see it was not part of Johnny's agenda.

Suddenly, I was officially in charge of the family budget. So, first things first. My top priority was to put good meals on the table and make sure the house payment was never late. It didn't take long to figure out that if I made the house payment plus the interest each month we would be rid of that payment sooner. Indeed, we paid off our Wallingford house in seven years—before any of the kids finished high school. That was a happy day.

When we lived on Woodlawn, World War II was still in full force. We were on strict rations for meat, butter, sugar, gas and other staples and no one wasted anything. It was a learning period for both of us, a time to consider carefully every purchase. To his credit, Johnny learned to trust my taking care of the finances. He did his part by being a faithful provider.

Johnny and I tried to show our kids by example how to manage resources carefully, and we taught them from little on how to handle any money they made running paper routes, doing lawns, working as mother's helpers or babysitting. As the oldest boys grew they were in high demand for their lawn work. When Jack and Jim had more customers than they could handle in the neighborhood, their dad began to help them after work and on the weekends.

Eventually, what started out as a childhood allowance scheme became a family enterprise, a landscaping and lawn care business, that over a period of 25 years passed from brother to brother, starting with Jack and Jim and on to Vince, Larry, David, Greg, Joe and Paul. Many of the original customers that started with Jack were still with the Schuler boys when Joe and Paul were the only "company workers." The boys all say that their dad taught them not only to make their best effort, but how to improve their skills and manage time efficiently.

During this period, the boys were able to earn their own Catholic school tuition. There was enough to cover fees at Blanchet High and Holy Names Academy—added to what the girls earned on service scholarships. While at O'Dea High School, Jack was able to retire from lawn work when he got an after-school job at McCann's Men's and Boys' Shop in downtown Seattle. The other boys also moved on to more ambitious goals during their high school years. Vince was a doorman at an upscale retirement home, David got a job at a restaurant, Larry worked for a construction company, and so on down the line.

In the early years when the kids were small, making ends meet was especially challenging. Yet, we always managed, sometimes through the generosity of others. I remember how grateful I was when a neighbor family gave me a large box of baby clothes and diapers. This was before Pampers existed, when cloth diapers were a necessity. Another dear lady asked if I would be offended if she offered me her eight-year-old daughter's collection of out-grown clothes. The camelhair coat with mittens, hat and leggings was the perfect size for my three-year-old—exactly what she needed—and she loved it. At that time, it seems everyone was sharing and we were delighted with hand-me-downs. I also discovered thrift shops. We were recycling before recycling was in vogue, and whether with store-bought clothes or hand-me-downs, my children were always well dressed.

I experienced many gestures of generosity over the years. One was unforgettable. I needed a new outfit for my fast-growing Joanie. This was about 1955. It was Easter, in the days when mothers loved to dress their little girls in something new and pretty for the Easter parade. With nine children, the demands on the clothing budget were enormous, and as usual I prayed for the impossible. Then, out of the blue came a $50 cashier's check in the mail. No name, just a typed note, "For whatever you need. No strings attached." I never had a clue about who sent it, but God knows, and I asked Him to bless that person. Throughout our family life I have experienced many such incidents of God's loving care.

Another one especially stands out, because it involved a group of twelve friends, members of Johnny's poker club. We were expecting our eighth baby in mid-February. In January, due to a slow time at Johnny's place of employment, a decision was made to rotate some days off. It was not welcome news to miss even a day's work. In that period, 1949, most wives were at home. Telephone visiting was a common break time and a means of expressing friendship, interest in each others kids and sharing of joys and struggles. So the word got out that Johnny was experiencing some lay-off time.

It was his turn to host the poker club that month, and as his buddies arrived, Johnny was in for a surprise. His poker evening turned out to be a "Baby Shower." The men, struggling to hide their amusement, presented him with a baby gift, a pretty crib blanket. Johnny smiled his thanks, a little surprised. His friends, enjoying his confusion, could hardly wait to announce "Johnny, we have a few more things," as they carried in two cases of Carnation milk, a fifty pound sack of potatoes, a case of oranges, a box of apples and a few other items. Finally, they presented the prize: the key to a freezer locker which contained a hind quarter of beef! This was truly a gift from heaven.

Johnny and I had such affection for these dear friends who built deep bonds of love and support for us and for each other through the years. I am the sole survivor of that extraordinary, loving group. Surely, those twelve men and their wives are now reaping their reward.

Baby David's birth was our first delivery that was covered by group insurance from Johnny's union and the birth of our baby was, as always, a blessed and happy event.

Christmas at the Schuler Home

Following our parents' German custom we always celebrated our Christmas gift exchange on Christmas Eve. It was the night that Santa came and it was the beginning of our Christmas holiday celebration.

During the Advent weeks just before Christmas, Johnny would be in his workshop in the basement making or fixing the special toys the kids would be getting on that magical moment of Christmas Eve. A skilled artisan, he recycled many a bike and tricycle over the years, and even fabricated his own toys. The most treasured toy Johnny created was the thirties-style tractor he made in 1949. Fashioned of steel, it came with several attachments, including a plow, a rake and even a harrow. Indestructible, it passed from one child to another for over twenty years.

Johnny's hand-crafted, indestructible toy
tractor and plow, now 62 years old.

The children at Sacred Heart Orphanage across town were also the beneficiaries of Johnny's creativity. He loved his "Santa" workshop projects and always looked forward to making Christmas special for them too, with refurbished tricycles, toy trucks and freshly painted wagons. He loved contributing this way and his Christmas joy was contagious!

Finding ways to hide my own efforts—often at the sewing machine—to make Christmas memorable for the kids took a bit of creativity at times. But after a trip to the doll hospital many a recycled "baby" would be magically outfitted with a new layette.

As Christmas Eve approached, excitement would reach a pitch around the house. There was much to do to pull it off and everyone participated in the preparations. The tree had to be up, the house cleaned and polished, packages wrapped, and food bought and ready for Christmas dinner the following day. Brooms and mops and the Old English furniture polish came out and everyone had a chore. The girls worked on cleaning the house, ironing tablecloths and getting "Sunday best" clothes ready for the holiday. Of course, there was always a designated "errand boy," who'd be dispatched to the corner store two blocks from the house more than once that day for various forgotten but needed items. Coming down to the wire, Johnny would be putting the finishing touches on his special projects and I'd still be wrapping my gifts.

Finally, after supper when all the work was done, our Christmas ritual began. The little ones knew Santa was on his way and would soon arrive. It was our challenge to make it happen without a hitch so that all the toys Santa brought would appear miraculously in the living room under the tree at just the right time.

But first we said the rosary and focused attention on the reason for our celebration. After the rosary we sang Christmas carols and had our "procession to the crib," a custom that began on our first Christmas in our home on Woodlawn in

1944. Singing "Silent Night," each child carried one figure to the crib. They chose from the statues of Joseph, Mary, shepherds, cows, angels, kings and camels. The youngest toddler always carried the baby Jesus. Once baby Jesus was safely asleep in his crib, it was time for the Santa Claus vigil.

I went into the kitchen with the kids while Johnny would slip out quietly to begin his task of being Santa. In the kitchen with the door to the dining room closed we sang carols and told stories. The obligatory reading of "The Night before Christmas," signaled the time to check and see if Santa had arrived.

It was always the littlest one who was sent into the dining room to peek behind the sliding double doors into the living room to discover if Santa had come. With a whoop of excitement, the doors opened wide and bedlam ensued as the rest of the kids entered the wonderland that Santa had left!

Another ritual of this magical night was the gift exchange. As the years went by and the kids began to earn from paper routes, mowing lawns, babysitting or running errands, they were able to save up for Christmas gifts. But when they were little they received a Christmas allowance to buy gifts for everyone in the family. One year, about a week before Christmas, Jack, 9, Marge, 7, Jim, 5, and Vince, 4, took their allowances and walked the seventeen blocks to the Wallingford Fuji's Dime Store on 45th Street to make their special purchases. The Fuji store was loaded with tempting items like figurines of birds and horses, harmonicas, and bells. At last they arrived home bursting with excitement over their choices. Then I heard Vince say, "Jimmy, if you tell what I got for Mommy I'm going to tell that you got Daddy a horse tooth brush." I quickly interrupted before this went any further. Imagine my amusement when Daddy unwrapped a long-handled nail brush. He didn't know why I was laughing.

During the week between Christmas and New Year's Day, Johnny took serious time to play with the kids. There were cozy evenings of Chinese checkers and Monopoly or playing with the model trains. Maybe it was a throwback to his years on the farm when the celebration of the holidays coincided with a lighter workload, but whatever the source, the holiday season always came with permission to relax and enjoy.

Over the years, Christmas Eve has continued to be a special night. To this day the extended family gathers for supper, carols, the procession to the crib and Santa, who now appears in person for the great grandchildren. In increasing numbers and currently to the fourth generation they come to what has become a Schuler Christmas Gala.

Now Grandma's house all festive with lights

Will welcome the family this cold winter night.

After hugging and feasting at Christmas buffet,

We'll place Baby Jesus in his crib filled with hay.

And singing the carols we learned long ago,

Then Jingle Bells, Jingle Bells and Ho, Ho, Ho.

Christmas Eve, 1958.

A spontaneous Christmas tableau performed by Larry, David, Rose Mary with baby Greg, and Joan, 1955.

The Christmas Eve procession to the crib.

The Circus

It was the second year we lived on Wallingford. The circus was coming to town. I knew the kids had never heard of the "Greatest Show on Earth," but recalling my childhood thrill at seeing the elephants, tigers and exciting stunts performed by wild animals, trapeze artists and tight rope walkers high up under the "Big Top," I promised that if we could raise the money we could all go. We just needed to raise the twenty dollars! Fortunately, that year, as every year, the crabapple tree produced more fruit than we needed. The kids were excited when I suggested that we package them, load them on their new wagon and go door to door to sell them. So we loaded lots of brown bags of crabapples and went door to door until the wagon was empty—and the money bag full. We counted the coins and the dollar bills, and we did it. "Kids, we are going to the circus!" They had never seen anything like that and oh, how they loved it.

The Soap Box Derby

Soon after we moved to Wallingford, Johnny heard about the "Soap Box Derby" and encouraged Jack to enter. It became an annual event in our house requiring endless hours of pains-taking construction of the racing cars, supervised by Daddy but built by the boys. When Jack was twelve he came within a couple of inches—a photo finish—of going to compete in Akron, Ohio on the famous Derby Downs race track. We were happy that he won a brand new Schwinn bicycle. Even though some friends had offered to drive to Ohio if he won, I knew it was impossible. Johnny would not be able to take the time off work and I would not have been able to leave the younger kids in any one else's care. So we were very happy for all the excitement of Jack's coming in at second place, his beautiful new bike, and being driven around the ball field in a special car at Rainier Stadium, home of Seattle Rainier's baseball team.

Jack and his soap box racer with all
his sibs, 1949.

Halloween

Halloween at the Schuler home was always a time of fun and creativity when the kids scrambled to make their costumes: everything from ghosts and witches to bandits, cowboys, cats and clowns. It all depended on what was available in the attic storage room. Over a period of more than 20 years we costumed kids of all ages, sizes and genders. We didn't always have a camera ready but the memories are bright and clear.

The year we decided to have a party for Margie's entire seventh grade class of 42 kids was the most fun. Her birthday was a few days before, so I got the invitations out early enough to give the mothers time to plan the costumes. And did they ever! One mom of twins made the prize winner, a Holstein cow. The costumes were hilarious. We decorated the house on three floors, a skeleton in the attic room lying on a pair of saw horses. The pantry was a fortune teller's booth. There was food in the kitchen and apple bobbing in the dining room. The mothers were helping me in every room and the kids had a great time.

Joan, Rose Mary and David all decked out for Halloween, 1958.

This was a special event because Margie finally had her own party. Every year another girl whose birthday was on the same day as hers always beat us to the date, inviting just a few friends. We made sure that everyone was invited and no one left out—and they all came. This group of kids, now in their seventies, still remember that amazing costume party.

Wheels

The Daddy of this family grew up with an unfulfilled dream of having a bicycle. He lived on his grandparents' farm in the country until the eighth grade when his mother bought a small house in the town of St. Marys close to St. Marys College campus where he went to the Jesuit prep school. But his dream of having a bike remained out of reach even while he was in high school and living in town with paved streets. Johnny never got his bike!

So once he got married and had a family, he could hardly wait to put his first son on a tricycle, then a bike. Eventually he had all the kids on wheels. He used his mechanical and artistic skills to re-create bicycles for everyone, including Mom and Dad, and for the babies who weren't big enough to ride, he

David and Greg on their bikes, 1963.

invented a bicycle trailer to attach to his bike. Often, on a summer evening the entire family would sail around Green Lake in a caravan of eleven bicycles and a baby trailer. We enjoyed it as spectators' heads spun around in surprise and astonishment.

A Family Vacation

It was 1957. Our eldest daughter, Marge, had graduated from Holy Names Academy in June and applied to join the Maryknoll Sisters of New York. She was scheduled for an interview with some of their Sisters in Stockton, California. We were busy trying to arrange that trip for her by train or bus. John's August vacation was on the calendar. We had a fairly new car and a new tent and were planning a camping trip to the ocean. It occurred to me that we may as well drive to California, camp when possible, and take some of the kids. The price of her ticket would cover the gas, and we'd have to eat even if we stayed home. Greg, going on three, was our youngest child. A friend offered to keep him for the week of our trip. Jack, Jim and Vince stayed home as they had their lawn work to cover.

So we headed off. Carol, David, Rose Mary and Joan shared the back seat. Everyone had a good time until we got to Stockton. The temperature was 117° Fahrenheit. We thought we would die! Marge finished her interview and we headed for San Francisco.

We visited Chinatown, rode the carousel in Golden Gate Park and played on the beach. The biggest excitement of the trip was experienced when a huge roller came crashing in and knocked David down as the wave washed over him. His brand new jeans and t-shirt were soaked! He scrambled to his feet with a look of shock I will not forget. It was not our first time to be on an ocean beach, but never before had we been that close to the surf. I am pleased to report that he was not permanently damaged, because he happily joined the Navy out of high school.

David, Carol, Rose Mary and Joan on the carousel at Golden Gate Park.

We spent a couple nights in a motel but mostly we camped. We were in awe of the giant redwood forest, the tallest trees in the world, and the beautiful blue Pacific spread out before us on the route home. In Oregon we stopped at the Rogue River and Gold Beach on the ocean. Along the coast we saw hundreds of sea lions and hiked down long trails to see these strange creatures. At every turn of the road a new vista lay before us. I wanted the children to feel awe at the beauty of God's Creation. My thoughts would often go back to my childhood in Kansas where I was always eager to know what was beyond my world but afraid I would never see it. And here it was, beauty beyond description: mountains, rivers and forests, fertile valleys, vineyards, orchards, fields of hay, logging trucks loaded and headed for mills, pastures filled with grazing cattle and flocks of sheep on grassy hillsides.

What a beautiful trip. But home we must go. There was school to prepare for, shopping to do, uniforms to get ready for the grade school and the girls' academy. For the older boys, attending Blanchet High meant "threads!" Of course, if Marge was accepted to Maryknoll, she would have a list of supplies that she'd need to gather. She passed up a full scholarship to attend Holy Names College in Spokane to carry out her plan to become a missionary Sister.

Loss

Returning from our early August vacation in 1957, I was fully aware that I was pregnant, feeling very sick and nauseated. I had never been this miserable this early in my pregnancies. Yet, there was so much work to be done. Besides school shopping, the garden was yielding a crop of green beans needing to be canned. Every evening Johnny would pick and stem a basketful and help me with the pressure cooker. At last we got the kids off to school, Jim and Vince to Blanchet High, Carol to Holy Names Academy, Larry, Rose Mary and David to St. Benedict's and Joan to McDonald kindergarten.

Then the Asian flu struck and Marge got very sick. Running a high fever she was too ill to take to the doctor but incredibly he made a house call. I stayed with her upstairs most of the time as I continued to battle morning sickness. Vince was also stricken with the flu. I made an effort to get meals on the table, but it was hard. After a couple of weeks Marge recovered and returned to her job at the Sears Catalog warehouse. The next day she had a relapse, this time with pneumonia, ending her job for good. This is when I came down with the flu. Two days later I felt suddenly better and relieved of the nausea. Gone! I was so thankful.

When Marge and I felt well again we shopped for her convent entrance "list" which included a black woolen sweater, black laced oxfords and other standard items such as black lisle hose, cotton underwear, toiletries—and a trunk to ship it all. We were gradually getting everything under control. It was now December and Marge was scheduled to leave home on the day after Christmas. First, she'd stop in Kansas to visit her Grandmothers. Then, on the day before New Year's Eve, she'd take the train to St. Louis and enter as a postulant at the Maryknoll Sisters novitiate in Valley Park. In the meantime there was much to do, but at least I was no longer sick.

On a Saturday morning December 5, 1957, we were getting ready to attend early Mass. I was looking forward to it as I had been too ill to go to church for a couple of months. Suddenly, I began to hemorrhage. There was no doubt that I was going to have a miscarriage. Johnny called my doctor who ordered me to the emergency room at Providence Hospital. In the meantime I passed out cold. Johnny got Jack and Marge to help get me to the car. This was before Seattle had Medic I units. Johnny had made seven trips to Providence Hospital for the birth of our babies, but he didn't know where the emergency entrance was so he took me to the front door as usual. In the meantime I gained consciousness and was put in a wheelchair to be admitted. I told the receptionist I needed to go to emergency, but she continued the routine questions, at which

time I fainted again. I remember it was 7 O'clock. When I gained consciousness again I heard the nurse who was pumping the BP monitor. "Still no BP, Doctor." He was furious because the blood had not yet arrived from the blood bank. Then I fainted again.

At 10:30 a.m. my doctor came in to tell me that my baby boy had died, perhaps two weeks ago. I recalled that I had the flu at that time and was running a high fever. He offered some soothing words about the loss, but I was sad because my baby didn't live to be baptized. At the same time I never doubted that his baby soul would be with Jesus.

I had three new units of blood flowing into my veins. The doctor kept me in the hospital three days for rest and recovery and when I got back home I felt energized. I was ready for all the demands of the next month, Christmas, and Marge's leaving home. I was aware that this could be a long separation if we did not carefully plan to visit her because at that time, pre-Vatican II, the rules did not include any vacations or trips home—and indeed, it was seven years before she returned for a visit. It bothered me that she had made this decision while so young. She had just turned 18 in October. So, it was with a little bit of "wait and see," and "God's will be done."

Christmas Day was a little sad but full of excitement too. The oven thermostat decided to terminate and when I checked the turkey at 10:30 a.m. it was overdone. The carcass had collapsed under full blast heat. Fortunately, it didn't burn or dry up and we ate early—the more time for board games. Friends and relatives stopped by to say good-bye to Margie. The next day we all accompanied her to the airport. She walked out on to the tarmac and we were all at the window waving to her as she climbed the stairs up to the big plane. She was the first one to leave home and the first of any of us to fly away. We will await her letters.

The Cook

Greg was a precocious child known for his early rising, enjoying breakfast with his daddy and then with a succession of the others as they came to the table. Greg learned to fry eggs when he was two going on three because I taught him. He always thought "anything you can do, I can do better," and cooking was there for the taking. I finally surrendered and taught him the right number to set for eggs and he faithfully did it standing on a chair by the stove, turner in hand and a plate ready to serve the next one to come to the breakfast table. When I baked I always gave him a ball of dough to knead or sugar cookies to dust. He was always there. One day when he was three, he climbed on the counter, opened the cupboard door searching for the Jell-O. I said, "No! You cannot make Jell-O! It takes boiling water and no mother in her right mind would let a three year old kid do that!" He said, "But I will make it with cold water." I replied, "No, that will not work." His rejoinder was something I will never forget, "Well, Mommy, let's say it like this, each of us knows how to cook." After all these years I still laugh when I recall that episode. As my only pre-schooler, we had a lot of quality time and great conversations.

Older brother Jim had an old Chevy that seemed to be in the "local repair shop" most of the time—our garage in the back,

of course, with the work being done by live-in mechanics. Greg called Jim's Chevy the "conk out car." When Greg was about four, Jim joined the National Guard and was assigned to Fort Gordon, Georgia, for his military training. His departure was a loss, particularly for little Greg whom he loved dearly.

About that time David and Larry were learning the Latin responses as they were preparing to become altar boys. Just for fun I taught Greg a couple of lines, and he caught on. So, we added a few more words. By the time Jim returned from Fort Gordon in a few months Greg was able to recite all the responses, including the "Confiteor."

Dad and the Boys

Johnny knew how to work, but also to play. He worked hard and he played hard—and he expected the kids to do the same. They used to tease him about his "German" approach to play that went something like this: "Dad thinks that when it's time to play, you're going to have fun whether you like it or not."

One of the main reasons for our choosing to live in the Northwest was Johnny's love of the great outdoors. Hunting

Johnny with five sons: Jack, Jim, Larry, Vince and Greg—with their dogs, guns and pheasants. Missing are David, who was in the Navy at the time, and Joe and Paul, who were too young to participate. About 1970.

and fishing were definitely his idea of great recreation, and he determined to teach his sons to love the bountiful forests, streams and fields as he did. Pheasant hunting, as well as scouting, biking, fishing, golfing and pigeon racing were just a few of the many activities the boys enjoyed with their father.

All of these experiences created deep bonds of camaraderie between Johnny and his sons, and among the brothers, even though the ages of the eight boys spanned 24 years.

Each son had his time with Dad.

Changes in the Church

Nineteen sixty-three was an exciting and interesting time in our family history as well as in national and world events, and in the Catholic Church. Vatican II, begun by Pope John XXIII was in its closing sessions under Paul VI. The death of John XXIII was mourned worldwide and the funeral televised. The biggest issue of the Council for the average Catholic parish was the new rule that Masses could be said in the vernacular, the local language, worldwide. Before that, it did not matter where in the world one attended Mass, it was in the Latin language, word for word. I personally welcomed this change. I loved to hear the words of Christ in the breaking of bread and visualize the institution of the Eucharist at the Last Supper when Jesus said, "This is my Body, this is my Blood. Do this in memory of Me." I knew it in the Latin form too, but hearing it in English made it so personal—and my future altar boys would not have to memorize the Latin responses. Also now, women and girls were allowed to be in the sanctuary as lectors or cantors and even be Eucharistic Ministers. The priest would be facing the congregation. All of the changes were a gift to me in that I felt it was easier to teach the children the mysteries and miracles of our Faith.

After our Pastor worked through the difficulties of the objections of some conservatives who were sure we were losing all that was holy, he named three couples to become Eucharistic Ministers. Johnny and I became one couple so privileged. We assisted with the distribution of the Sacred Bread on Sundays and during the week at daily Mass we were "sacristans," preparing the altar, laying out vestments, arranging the gifts of bread and wine. After two years there were more lay people appointed.

This was a happy time for me. Our "baby" was nearing school age, older kids had left home, I had my first car and for the first time felt a little freedom. I had charge of shopping for all of our needs. If I made a trip to the grocery store I could stop for a short "visit" as I passed St Benedict's. Throughout my life up to then I had never entered the church without a head covering. Of late it was popular to use a mantilla—a short lace veil. One day I did not have any head covering with me, and there was nothing in the vestibule. I didn't want to leave and made the decision to go in anyway, but felt uncomfortable. I was begging pardon when I heard clear words (somewhere in my head) "I love you with or without a veil." I think it almost took my breath away. Need I say, it was very liberating.

The Mission Guild

Throughout my busy life I can't think of anything that I would consider a hobby. I enjoyed reading and music; movies were rather rare. If I found time, I wrote letters and loved to receive them. At different times I corresponded with missionary priests and sisters: they were my heroes. As a child my parents subscribed to "The Field Afar," the original Maryknoll magazine. As soon as I could read, that was my favorite place to explore "faraway places with strange sounding names." Some of our Benedictine teachers also inspired us to love the missions and encouraged us to make little sacrifices to help in their support. Eventually, we had a family friend who was a Jesuit missionary to Japan. After World War II Japan experienced very hard times, and any little help we could send was so welcome. Often, we would invite friends to card parties to raise funds, and in the summer have fund-raising tea parties in the back yard. Our family also saved pennies for the missions.

At some point a few girl friends got together and thought it would be fun to create a little "guild" to see what we could do to help. They were from several other parishes and a few from St. Benedict's. At our first planning meeting we decided: "no dues, no officers, just get together, have fun, meet twice a month, save pennies and see what happens."

Little did we know where it would lead us. We never dreamed so many doors would open. One of the members knew a seaman who would be willing to transport a few boxes to Yokohama. St. Vincent De Paul's Jimmy Sakamoto asked us to help a priest in India and offered to transport a bolt of material if we could supply it. This led to gathering pennies in serious amounts. The elderly priest in India became our project. We sent the material for his teaching sisters to make new scapulars only to learn that he still needed to supply the exorbitant fee of three dollars before he could get the fabric out of customs. Just a few more pennies will help.

With time, enthusiasm and new members, we gave ourselves a name. We now called ourselves the "Missionaries of the Little Flower." Some of our members were converts and loved learning about the saints, especially, St. Therese. Through our Jesuit friend in Japan we became acquainted with a newly established order, the Sisters of St. John Evangelist. They had an orphanage in Tokyo. When our seaman reached Yokohama he contacted the Sisters and they were able to get in touch with some American soldiers who could pick up the boxes of clothes we had gathered. At some point, someone got the idea to collect the returned children's shoes from Nordstrom's— then just a Seattle shoe store. The big boxes of children's shoes, which we acquired from the store, were sorted and then shipped to the orphanage. God bless Nordstrom! During the Korean War, the Maryknoll Sisters were running a clinic, attending to thousands of refugees and rescuing abandoned babies. We managed to send clothing and boxes of homemade soap to their mission in Pusan.

There seemed to be plenty of opportunities to be helpful. As time went on we hosted luncheons here in my home. We usually served about forty guests. "No charge—just give what you can." It was well worth the effort. We also made crafts and held a bazaar.

As time went on our home obligations prevented us from doing as much as we did initially. Some of us were still having babies and some had teenagers. I had both challenges. At some point we retired the group but I continued with the correspondence. The "mission guild" period of my life was a was a time I will always treasure. I especially value the dear friends who worked so cheerfully and spread their enthusiasm to other friends who supported our work.

Recently I learned that a project we supported in the 1970s, the restoration of an irrigation system, is still supplying water to a plantain grove, and needed income to the school and parish in India. It is a joy to know that the work we started so many years ago continues to show results even now.

A Trip to Kansas

My mother's 80th birthday on October 3, 1965 was approaching. I had a happy thought that I could take Paul, who had not started kindergarten yet, and go by train to Topeka to celebrate my mother's 80th birthday with my siblings. My sister, Agnes, who lived in Port Angeles, Washington, had two little girls, Erin and Kerry, also preschoolers. When I proposed the idea to Agnes to go with me, she said she'd have to ask her husband, Don. I think she knew without asking that her chances were slim, as he would not like his routine interrupted. Sure enough, the answer was in the negative but the excuse was "no, we cannot afford it." Agnes said she was going to pray for a miracle. She really wanted to go. As the time approached, I'd call her to see if she had made any progress on her miracle. If anything, things had gone from bad to worse and the final word was a definite, "No." She'd had a car accident—her fault—and, of course, Don was upset with her. The repair had to be done.

Prior to this our little mission group had been gathering pennies and doing what we could to support an orphanage in South India. The elderly pastor was able to purchase American bulgur wheat at a low cost to feed the children. Then I got a letter from him desperately asking for more help because for

Our three youngest: Joe, Greg and Paul, 1965.

some diplomatic issue America had put an embargo on the shipment of the grain. Now he had to purchase it on the black market. Could we possibly send $50?

Just that morning I was asked why I never went to our parish bingo games on Saturday nights. "The jackpot is up to $640 and we have a $50 intermission blackout." I was doing the dinner dishes, thinking about the letter when it struck me: I might at least try for the $50, but it was nearing eight and I still had to return the freshly ironed surplices to the sacristy. Even with rushing as fast as I could I arrived at the bingo game at half time. They wouldn't allow me to play the intermission game, but for half price I could join the rest of the games.

At the jackpot blackout game, the final of the night, a miracle happened. Bingo! In 52 calls. They were stunned. I was stunned. I had won the $640! When I got home at nearly 11:00 p.m. I called Agnes to announce to her that she was going to go with me to Topeka. But she still had to get permission from the "boss."

"Well, go tell him." She came back to the phone giggling.

"Well, what did he say?" He said, "I guess you are going because this is bigger than we are."

The following Thursday we boarded the train with our three kids and arrived in Topeka in time to celebrate on Sunday.

With David, Larry, Johnny, Joe, Greg and Paul, 1966.

117

Mother's Day, 1958 Back: Johnny, Carol, Jack, and Jim.
Front: David, Joan, me, Rose Mary, Larry, and Vince
holding Greg.

Even my oldest brother, Brother Paul, from St. Benedict Abbey at Atchison appeared suddenly from hiding. What a happy reunion. All of us living siblings and a lot of relatives came. My mom was so happy. It was a surprise to her and she loved it. Agnes was sure it was her prayers that were answered and dear Father Sousainather in a village in India must have been overjoyed with the benefits of my winnings from Bingo. And I, for sure, believe in miracles—a blackout in 52 calls!

I appreciated my win, of course, but it came with a reminder. On Monday morning following the win, I went to the church office to pick up the cash prize. About noon I was spreading it out on the dining table: rail tickets for Agnes and me, food for a couple of days on the train for the five of us, one half of it could go to India (after all, I went to win $50 for the orphanage and would have sent it all had I won the $50). And we were given all this abundance. Just then, the doorbell rang and there stood a most pathetic man in rags begging to clean my flowerbeds for a little money. I was a little "shook." That was the first time I'd ever had a beggar at my door. We were taught to see Christ in the poor, so what was I to think? I will let you figure that out! Come to think about it, he really didn't beg but

My sister Agnes, my brother Bud, and I.

offered to work. So, I told him to do a small flowerbed and gave him a couple bills—and quickly gathered the cash to stash. I will have to say I was a little nervous. When I was a child we frequently had "hobos" at the door begging for food. My mother always found something to serve because if it wasn't Jesus Himself, it surely was the "least of His brethren." And if that wasn't enough to motivate us to share, one of my Dad's favorite quotes comes to mind, "But for the Grace of God, there go I."

The Piano

My dream of having a musically talented family wasn't going too well. I had met and become friends with a retired professional pianist. She and her husband had moved here from Chicago. They had no children of their own but as we grew to know each other they soon took an interest in our children. One day the conversation was about music and how up to then we had not been able to see our way to get a piano and start anyone in music lessons. She encouraged us to look for a used piano and then she offered to give Margie free lessons.

And it happened. We did find a bargain—missing a couple of ivories—but with a beautiful tone. Unfortunately, that same year, 1952, we purchased our first television. Before we realized it there was no hope for the piano. The living room was filled with kids from all over the neighborhood watching TV. What with homework and other activities the piano soon stood idle. And my friend moved to California. End of music for Margie. Next Carol, no interest. Next came Rose Mary who did very well with music lessons at the local Dominican convent. She was eight when she started. About this time, her sister, Joanie, five years younger discovered a gift. She could play by ear.

Joan began playing at age three and spent hours at the piano never seeming to hit a sour note. Composing her own works she discovered chords and tunes to musically tell a story. For instance, playing some "angry" sounds, she tells us: "That's King Herod telling the three wise men to go find Jesus." The oriental rhythmic sounds were "the camels going across the desert" and the twinkling high notes were "the stah." (She had a problem pronouncing "r"s.) And when they found Jesus and adored him, the music made me cry.

All this was followed by formal music lessons, reading notes, lots of finger work and perhaps a de-emphasis on creativity,

Rose Mary and Joan playing the piano, 1960.

but the lessons went on with different teachers over the years. During her last three years of studying music at Holy Names Academy she developed a great repertoire of Chopin and other classical piano composers. Rose Mary and Joan both continued to play over the years, bringing the family many hours of musical entertainment. So, even though my kids didn't turn out to be the "Trapp Family Singers," they did bring music into our home, making the sacrifice to buy that old beat-up piano pay off in the end.

The Baptismal Gown

It started as a plain white dress, made by his grandmother for Jack's baptism in 1937, and it ended up a tradition. Knowing that all twelve Schuler babies had been baptized in the same simple little white dress of fine batiste, new parents Vince and Mary Ann requested it for their first-born. I was touched by their appreciation of its history, especially that it

My youngest son Paul, Nadine and their baby, Nathan, in the Schuler baptismal gown, 1998.

was made by Grandma Margaret Schuler, their baby Kristen's great grandmother. To make it a little more festive, we added a row of lace at the hem. After that it was used by all of the grandchildren. It grew in length with each addition of lace for each baptism and became a treasured icon. After the last grandson, Nathan, wore it in 1998 it was retired. If there were a Schuler museum, the 74 year-old, now fragile baptismal gown would surely be found there.

Pilgrimage

It was the year of "Jubilee," Holy Year 1975. In March we learned that a pilgrimage to Lourdes and Rome with more than a thousand Marriage Encounter couples was being planned for October. The price was reasonable, and we had six months to prepare. From the day Johnny and I decided to go I was in a state of excitement at the thought of going to Rome. And it all came true. We flew non-stop to New York, boarded an Alitalia airliner for a night flight to Lourdes, France. A bus took us to the grotto.

Even though it was late October the entire enclosure was crowded with people from around the world. I had promised my brother who was in the last stages of colon cancer that I would enter the baths for him. He was so sure he would be cured he told his family "I will be home in late October." In the brief moments that I was in the icy water every joint in my body was in sharp pain. Then the assistants helped me up, put a robe on me and I was instantly dry and warm. Oscar died shortly after. He did go home—to God.

Now onto Rome by train, much of it in view of the blue water of the Mediterranean Sea. Rome at last! I can't even try to describe the wonder: awesome St. Peter's, Mass with Pope Paul VI in the Square, the three other basilicas, the Coliseum, the fountains, the sculptures and paintings, ancient ruins, the Catacombs. "I must be dreaming." There followed an overnight trip to Venice where we danced at midnight to violin music coming from somewhere behind the pillars surrounding the Piazza. We returned to Rome for our departure, filled with gratitude for this wonderful trip.

Deo Gratias.

Mary Lou

Springtime, 1967. It was Easter, a time for new beginnings, a time for joy and hope. But that year I experienced grief. I didn't know I had so many tears. My dearest friend had died suddenly of a heart attack at just 35 years of age. Our friendship had grown through the years. We were in almost daily contact. Whether it was greetings at early morning Mass or drop-in visits or phone conversations, contact with Mary Lou was always enjoyable. Her sense of humor, her deep spirituality, her heart as big as her overweight body, made her the most loving, giving person I ever knew.

A favorite story Mary Lou told about her six year-old son says much about her, too. Matthew went to the local drug store (also a gift shop) to choose his mother's birthday gift. When he brought a lovely vase to the counter, the friendly proprietor asked him if he knew it cost $20. Innocently, Matthew said, "Oh, I don't have any money. My mommy says all the best things are free."

Her efforts at weight loss were extreme but unsuccessful. Our last conversation foretold her death. She sadly said to me, "Dorothy, I'm not going to make it." It was hard for me. I had lost my best friend, Mary Lou.

So who comes to my rescue? My caring daughter, Carol. She had just bought an almost new, bright red Volkswagen "Beetle," her first car. "Mom, let's drive down the coast. How about San Francisco?"

And off we went. We had a wonderful time. We visited friends, dined at Fisherman's Wharf, enjoyed some tourist attractions and headed home refreshed with lots of good memories.

And I was comforted to know that the memory of my friend, Mary Lou, would continue to cheer me up as she had all through the years.

CHAPTER NINE
ANDERSON ISLAND

The Dream

"Pinewood" was an impossible dream that came true. The dream began when Margie was at Holy Names Academy, and a friend invited her to vacation with her family at Dogwood, their summer home on Nisqually Reach at the south end of Puget Sound. She came home with endless stories of the fun and adventures of life in the woods and on the shores of Puget Sound: wading out into the cold waters to capture as many Dungeness crabs as needed for the evening feast, clam digging at low tide, beach combing, storytelling, fun and games with the Hilling family at their place called Dogwood. While there she also painted in oils the surrounding scenes of mountains, sea and islands. I could only hope she would be invited again.

Years passed since Margie's experience at a summer home on the Sound. She had graduated from Holy Names Academy and entered the Maryknoll Sisters. Little sisters Carol and Rose Mary had grown up and married as had Jack, Jim, Vince and Larry. David joined the navy and Joan was a junior at Holy Names Academy. Time and circumstances had changed. We added two little boys after Marge left home. Now it was Joan, Greg, Joe and Paul at home. At that time I was providing daycare for a neighbor family of seven kids while their mother returned to her career as a social worker. At long last I was able to contribute a little earning to the family income. Actually, I saved every penny of it to start a retirement fund.

125

Then something happened to bring many new surprises into our life. A friend and neighbor invited us to take a tour of a new development on a three by five mile island in Puget Sound. She had seen it, loved it, bought a parcel of land and could earn a $25 credit by showing it to other prospective buyers. My husband reluctantly agreed to go but didn't like the prospect of listening to a sales pitch for something he was sure was beyond our means. It turned out to be a lovely day and he fell in love with Anderson Island, the southern-most island in Puget Sound, and all it had to offer. The salesperson assured us of the joys we would realize with a family membership in the Riviera Country Club: a nice campground, all that beautiful blue water we saw, the sprouting golf course and the blooming dogwood trees. It was just beautiful! The offers got better. "Buy today and get $400 off. There'll be only a $50 a month payment after a $600 down payment—and you can earn $25 for each new prospect or $100 if they buy a lot." At that point I told Johnny I had the $600, saved from the daycare money. He was nearly in tears. He kept saying, "The kids would love it." And it was plain to see that he, too, was loving it.

The younger children: David, Joan, Greg and baby Joe.

The "Island"

In just three years we owned our lot free and clear, had bought a travel trailer to replace that awful army tent and were enjoying the wonders and beauty of an island in the Sound. The married kids had pickup trucks with canopies for sleeping. They were all acquiring sets of golf clubs—mostly from the St. Vincent de Paul Salvage Bureau on Lake Union—and riding across on the little ferry boat that only held nine cars. It didn't take long to make that ferry obsolete as more and more week-enders were discovering Anderson Island.

The island was settled around 1850 by several Scandinavian immigrants, and when we purchased our little piece of land in the development called the "Riviera," there was still some farming going on at the southern end, some chicken coups, orchards, logging, and fewer than 150 year-round residents. The few original Indian dwellers had left or died and folks with names like Johnson, Carlson and Anderson were suddenly fearful of what was happening to their precious peaceful private island life. It didn't take long for us to share their feelings. The nine-car ferry was replaced with one with a 38-car capacity and the ferry lines began to grow longer. Our ferry boat also serviced little Ketron Island and McNeil island, so it wasn't exactly a lot of service in the first place. But the Schulers were undaunted. It was a 50 mile trip from our home

in Seattle to the Steilacoom ferry dock and a half hour ferry ride to Anderson Island.

Almost everyone in the family was learning to play golf and it was obvious that some of the brothers were naturals. Johnny had learned the game as a student at St. Marys College, which had a golf course. He hadn't played since we left St. Marys, so he was happy to pick it up again after 30 years and introduce his sons to the sport. The Anderson Island nine-hole executive golf course was beautiful and challenging. To me, its best feature was the peaceful quiet under beautiful blue skies. It took only one good putt or drive to bring us back for another round hoping for that perfect shot. Eventually it happened to Johnny—a hole in one. Witnessed! A couple of years later, we felt comfortable playing in foursomes. We happily watched the family members improve their game—and their equipment.

After four years we were still camping in the campground. The sons and daughters, spouses and grandchildren were enjoying "our" island with its lakes, tennis courts, parks, island back roads and endless saltwater beaches on the Sound. Some of the kids were learning to water ski on Lake Florence and dive off the dock. Lake Josephine was off limits to motors, but there were plenty of reasons to launch a row boat or small sail boat.

Camping before the house was built.

When we purchased the lot in the woods near the southern end of Lake Josephine by a swimming beach, we had no intention of building a house on our lot. Johnny was 63 years old, and we had four kids in school. Joan was a junior at Holy Names Academy. Greg, Joe, and Paul were still in grade school at St. Benedict's. Four years later we were at ground zero again with regard to our retirement fund.

On weekdays I was very busy with daycare but tried to line up weekend prospects. Each one got a lovely breakfast and a boat ride to Anderson Island to hear the sales pitch and I got a $25 credit on our contract. Once, I earned $100 for a sale. My daycare income increased after I became licensed and had a full quota of children: two babies under two and four others. I immediately began to replace my savings fund and several years later had saved over $30,000, but still we had no thought of building. Our concern was preparing for retirement and maintaining our home in Seattle, which we had no intention of leaving. Of course, our family continued to grow with grandchildren expanding our numbers. And everyone enjoyed our trips to the island.

Pinewood

There were lots of houses being built on wooded lots like ours and finally we began to talk about the possibility of building. In 1975 Marge spent vacation with us camping on the island. Where else? Bev and Jim were there with their two little boys as well. During that week Marge and Bev inquired about what would be involved and the potential cost of constructing a cabin. Suddenly we realized that with our workforce and some of my savings we could put a house on our lot. Vince, who was by then a journeyman carpenter, drew a plan that answered our requests—a living room that would handle at least three card tables, a kitchen with a dinette and at least three bed-rooms, a bath and a laundry room. We were soon in the process of getting plans approved, felling trees to clear the lot and obtaining bids on materials and installations. We fell heir to a set of pre-built rafters which was a windfall to us. It was exciting to see all the details being worked out. It seemed everyone had some special way to contribute. Sorting and selecting cabinets from a remodel job to the exact needs of our kitchen was Dad's project. Vince, the supervisor, borrowed the foundation forms from his boss's construction company and scheduled the foundation preparation on a 3-day week-end in February. From then until the end of May every detail was carefully planned.

The entire family, camping out in trailers, campers or tents, was on the job early on a rain soaked Saturday morning of Memorial Day weekend, 1977. Vince announced the schedule. On Saturday the floor would be complete by 8 AM. The sidewalls, including windows and insulation, would be constructed and raised by noon. On Sunday the roof would go up; on Monday, the doors hung. Greg, running our Super 8 home movie camera, recorded this Memorial Day "barn raising" event. What began early Saturday morning with nothing but a concrete foundation ended by Monday evening as a house complete with a fully shingled roof and a front

Clearing the lot, getting ready to build.

door that closed and locked. There amid the stately evergreen firs was a house! "Schuler's Pinewood." A dream come true.

Next came the interior: installation of wiring, plumbing, drywall, kitchen cabinets and appliances made the house almost functional, but oh, the hours of work it would still require. Completing the painting, tiling, carpeting, and many other necessary details soon made our "cabin in the woods," a comfortable and welcoming get away.

Over the years the family's ties to Anderson Island strengthened to the point that it became an important anchor binding the growing family together. Several family members built their own homes on the island. Holidays often find them there enjoying each other's company for a round of golf, going on a fishing or crabbing jaunt or sitting around a campfire in the evening. The "John Schuler Memorial Golf Tournament" has been a staple of Labor Day weekends for over twenty years. In 1991 and again in 2003 elaborate Family Reunions brought the generations together for three days of fun. Activities included not only golf, but bike rallies, treasure hunts, boat races, hiking and barbeques.

And as Johnny so sweetly predicted, the "kids" did love it.

"Schuler's Pinewood"

1991 Family Reunion.

Reunion games:

Golf, "crazy" row boat races, and a bike rally.

Here we are, all decked out as pirates for the Anderson Island annual Labor Day parade during our 2003 Family Reunion. Grandson Martin is "Captain Jack Sparrow." Son Greg's smoking canon was a big hit.

2003 Family Reunion. Here I am with all my children, most of my grandchildren, great grandchildren and spouses of various generations.

CHAPTER TEN
A SPECIAL REMEMBRANCE

Arise, My Love

"Arise, my love, my dove, my beautiful one, and come. The winter is past, the rains are over and gone—and the fish are jumping in Jamison Lake! "

So announced my husband one morning in early May, 1986, and then he informed me that he had made reservations at the resort.

"We will spend the night at Carol and Tony's in Wenatchee and meet Bud and Marion at the lake."

If he thought I was going to give him any excuses, he was wrong. It sounded wonderful to me. Leisure time to fish, play bridge, visit, and pray together. He was really excited about his plan, and I assure you, when he made a phone call without even asking me to do it, it had to be very important to him. But sometimes the best laid plans are changed. A phone call came from Marion to say she was ill and that they would not be able to meet us at the lake. I was so disappointed. I said a quick prayer, "Dear Lord, this is not going according to our plan. Please take over."

Not only was I disappointed to be deprived of Bud and Marion's company, but because our dear friends' presence would have been a security blanket for me. I lived with the fear of Johnny's heart condition. Having been warned of the possibility of a massive coronary after his first heart attack nearly five years earlier or of another episode of congestive heart failure, which we had experienced many times, I was a little frightened to go off on the trip alone. However, our confidence had grown with the passing of nearly two years without a trip to the emergency room, which was usually followed by a few days in the hospital.

At this point nothing was going to change our plans. The outboard motor, fishing gear, bait, our food and sleeping bags were loaded in the station wagon. Johnny's spirits were high; his heart was set on this fishing trip. I couldn't disappoint him, though frankly, once we arrived in Wenatchee, I would have been happy to stay in town with Carol, Tony and the grand-kids. So off we went on that lovely morning in apple blossom time. We drove through miles of apple orchards sweet with the scent of the blossoms. We crossed the Columbia River, and then we traveled north.

Gaining altitude, I was enjoying scenery that I had never encountered before. Up through the canyon we drove and suddenly it seemed we were on top of the world. Below was a view of a picturesque small town with old frame houses, churches, a town hall and a big windmill. When we were almost through the town of Waterville, we noticed a Catholic Church with a number of cars in the parking lot. It being exactly nine o'clock, it occurred to us that Mass was about to begin. A quick U turn, and minutes later we joined a group of farmer's wives and others to attend Mass.

Since this was our daily habit we felt so blessed to be there. There was even a visiting priest concelebrating with the old pastor. After Mass we were invited to join these friendly folks for coffee. The ladies were looking forward to a demonstration of Mexican food preparation. When the Pastor learned that we were on a fishing trip, he gave us a special blessing for a safe trip, and "limits" of fish.

So we traveled on, very aware that my prayer was being answered. We drove east for many miles through what seemed like the biggest lawn in the whole world—endless

fields of young, very green wheat. We could only visualize what it would be like in a few months: taller and golden under a hot summer sun, the wind creating an ocean on dry land, waves and waves of glistening grain, dancing, waiting to be harvested. This is desert land, but drenched with the irrigating waters of the mighty Columbia, the formerly dry land now produces wheat. After many miles we passed through sagebrush and hundreds of blooming lupines, then the cutoff to Jamison Lake, my first and last trout fishing trip with Johnny.

What a surprising sight it was. Two separate lakes, one with high cliffs on the western side. Arriving at the resort, we soon had the key to our cabin. To say it was rustic would be a compliment. Oh well, we were never used to luxury vacations. This was a lot better than a tent. So we rented a boat, hitched on our outboard motor and made our way across the lake. We drifted around in the shadow of the cliffs, watching eagles soaring overhead in the clear, blue sky. To Johnny, who loved the out of doors and any "hunting" sport, this was the ultimate dream of a Kansas farm boy. We anchored, baited our hooks, and soon the fun began.

Nibbles, strikes, some boated, some lost, some keepers, some thrown back. Casting out, reeling in, tangled lines, lively fish flashing silver as they broke water. What fun we were having, and indeed it was a successful run. We had our two limits as the sun disappeared behind the cliff. A brisk wind came up and we were glad to return to shore. Now we had a big task ahead. Cleaning sixteen trout in an outdoor sink with a cold wind blowing, we questioned why we didn't throw them back. We soon discovered there were others who hadn't been so lucky. So we had the enjoyment of sharing our catch with several groups of campers and disappointed fishermen— thinking we could repeat the fun the next day.

We went to our cabin, thawed out by the little gas heater, cooked and feasted on that delicious trout. After our dinner we played our usual rubber of cribbage, and decided it had been a long and lovely day. We talked for hours recalling different trips, and other events in our lives. Good times, bad times, tough and joyful times; good decisions, bad mistakes. We both agreed we had never felt closer to God, or to each other. We were especially grateful to God for the time we'd had since Johnny's first heart attack five years ago. We were enjoying each day and each other.

Eleven years earlier, on our 38th wedding anniversary Johnny and I made a Marriage Encounter retreat. We both came away with a renewed awareness of the presence of God in our married life. Because it was January and the retreat center was high and deep in the Cascade Mountains of Washington we were not sure we would survive the unheated rooms. But as we stood around the altar at the closing Mass and sang the beautiful "Come back to me with all your heart," we knew our future had just begun. Like tall trees in the wind we would bend for each other.

My husband was a rather quiet man, a characteristic notice-able in groups, whether social or task-oriented. He was satisfied to let others do the talking. Not that he didn't have a lot to offer, he just held back. He did have opinions but often only shared them with me.

When he attended St. Marys College High School, the Jesuit prep school in St. Marys Kansas, he'd had a rather difficult time—so he always told me. He didn't enjoy classes domi-neered by the bright young boarding students from all over the U.S., who treated the non-boarding local boys, or "day dogs," as second class citizens. He had a slight stutter when he was nervous. But all in all he came out with an excellent prep school education emphasizing language, (English, Latin, and Spanish) science and math and lots of history. Most of all he was deeply, beautifully formed, a highly principled, consci-entious man who loved his Catholic faith and lived it. Of course, he was influenced by his male dominated upbringing in ways that he was unaware of until the years mellowed him with wisdom and understanding—a fringe benefit of raising twelve children over a period of forty-five years.

Only recently had I discovered the beautiful "Song of Songs" in the Bible. I teased Johnny because all those years when he would call me "my love, my dove, my beautiful one" I thought it was original. Somehow, through all our life together, no other term of endearment touched my heart, as did his "Good morning, my love." When he wasn't rushing off to work or to some other project, and had the rare luxury of leisure time, he would add the rest of the words, memorized from his high school days with the Jesuits.

Morning broke to the sound of wind whistling, bending the trees and turning Jamison Lake into a sea of white caps. It was a quick mutual decision to return to Wenatchee. Without even checking the time we loaded our gear. As I did the final cleanup, Johnny went to the store to cancel the rest of our reservation. While there he read and made a copy of "The Sportsman's Prayer."

Back through the sage covered desert we flew through the clear, exhilarating air. Soon we were back at the spectacular

sight of those green fields of wheat under the blue sky, and then we were, once again, in the little town of Waterville. It was exactly nine o'clock. This time there was a single car in the church parking lot. We entered the church just as Mass began. Only two old ladies were in attendance.

A feeling of joy and happiness filled my soul as I meditated on the gift of love. Kneeling there beside my faithful husband, I felt so blessed by God for the unexpected gift of Eucharist that day. (Dare I think that He sent the wind to churn the lake and send us back to this most special Mass and Communion together?) The words of the poem, scattered parts, poorly remembered, sang through my mind and heart:

"Hark, My lover comes, springing across the mountains, leaping across the hills. My lover belongs to me and I to him."

Beside him here, whom my heart loves, I hear his song:

"Arise, my love, my dove, my beautiful one.
The winter is past, the rains are over and gone,
and the flowers appear on the earth,
the time for pruning has come,
and the song of the dove is heard in our land. "
     Song of Solomon 2:10-14

Farewell

A week later the massive coronary occurred. Johnny died suddenly Friday, at noon, May 9th, 1986, at home, in my arms. We had spent a lovely morning attending Mass, then shopping for our spring supply of bedding plants, the dozens of multi-colored impatiens for the border bed around the front porch. He told me he had placed them in the shelter of the eaves and would not plant them until the ground warmed up in a few weeks. We had planned to meet friends in downtown Seattle, but once again our plans were changed. There were three other friends who had a standing invitation to meet Johnny at his final hour on this earth, and this was the day they chose to call. "Jesus, Mary and Joseph, I give you my heart and my soul, Jesus, Mary and Joseph be with me in my last hour, Jesus, Mary and Joseph may I breathe forth my soul in peace with You." Without fail, he said this prayer every night. Throughout his long life, that would have been thousands of invitations. I am sure they accepted, and were there.

When the available family had gathered we formed a procession, and borne by his children Johnny left his home of thirty-eight years and his grieving family. His funeral the following Tuesday was a wonderful celebration of his life. Friends and family filled the church to overflowing for the funeral Mass. Johnny's pall bearers were his twelve children and his grandsons the altar servers.

His casket was filled with notes and treasures. Damian had recently earned his Eagle Scout badge and that went with Grandpa, as well as a full set of Seattle Mariners baseball cards, a pheasant feather and other precious mementos from the grandchildren. Someone put in a fishing lure with the memory of "Opening Day" on Green Lake when Dad would take the kids at dawn. So many precious memories. The parish choir sang and Rose Mary presented the eulogy. With input from all the family, the eulogy emphasized Johnny's faithfulness and unconditional love. "He didn't preach, but lived his faith."

Eulogy of John Schuler, May 13, 1986

There is a season...A time for every purpose under heaven
A time to be born...

Dad was born in Kansas on October 27, 1906, the only son of German immigrant parents. Dad's own father died when he was an infant. He lived with his mother, a sister and several aunts and uncles on the family farm. This Kansas farm boy was schooled until 8th grade in a one-room country school and then by the Jesuit Fathers at a college prep school in St. Mary's, Kansas. There, he coupled his working skills with scholarship and honed the virtues of a Christian gentleman.

It was at a church bazaar that Dad mustered the courage to chat with a pretty, blue-eyed, strawberry blonde, named Dorothy Meinhardt. A year later John Schuler, then 30, and Dorothy were married in the steepled stone church in St. Mary's, Kansas.

By the late 1930's, young farmers were leaving for the city to seek new livelihoods. Mom and Dad recognized the instability and bleak future of farming and sensed a yearning to come to the Northwest and raise their family in the city. With the blessing and assurance of their parish priest that there were "saints in the city, too," they left Kansas with the proceeds of their farm sale and came to Seattle, finding their home in the natural beauty of the Northwest and here in St. Benedict's Parish 43 years ago.

A Time for Faith...

It goes without saying that the fullness of Dad's life was the wholeness he found with our mother and with his faith. Their strong beliefs and love sustained them through the good times and the bad. Dad's personal faith was simple. He was not a "preacher." He really never talked about religion; he simply lived the gospel he believed. He nurtured his children in the same faith-life through Catholic education and example. Dad was open and grew with changes in the Church. He valued the faith experience of his Cursillo and his participation in Marriage Encounter and the St. Vincent de Paul Society. He felt it a great honor to be a Eucharistic Minister.

The gospel value that superseded all others was his unconditional love.

A Time to Grow...

Dad wasn't always a big ol' Teddy Bear. He had a strong dose of German stubbornness and temper. He was a strict disciplinarian. Unlike today, he believed that "to spare the rod was to spoil the child." There are no spoiled Schulers! But what we knew most is that while he reprimanded us, his love for us was not dependent on our perfect behavior. We did mess up but Dad grew in depth and understanding because of it. He never stood in judgment, he just loved us.

The good side of Dad's impatience was that he got things done! Dad was a working-man all of his life. He never missed work and did not retire until he was 74 years old. He did not strive for wealth but provided us with all the material things we needed. Beyond his own craft, he was a skilled artisan in so many ways, a "jack of all trades and master of many." He had an ability to adapt his innate skills to the needs at hand and he was proud of his accomplishments, large or small. It was that very sense of responsibility and pride in his work that Dad instilled in all of his children, not just sons but daughters as well. At an early age all of us shared the work-load of family life: whether in daily chores or mowing lawns and babysitting to help earn our Catholic school tuition, we all participated.

Dad was proud of all of us in our life work, he respected the value and place each one of us had in the world.

A Time to Play...

Dad did take time to play, but only when the work was done. He wasn't satisfied to just admire the beauty of this land but rather he explored all of the possibilities of experiencing it in simple ways, from family bike rides around Green Lake to camping in the mountains; even once a special pilgrimage to Duvall to hand carry river rock to build a backyard fishpond. Dad dearly loved his flowers and his rock garden.

He loved to hunt and especially to fish. On Opening Day many a Schuler child secretly slept in full fishing gear and rubber boots so as not to miss Dad's 5 A.M. fishing call for Green Lake. He liked baseball and a good game of cards: he made a deck of cards dance from a penny ante poker game to a serious round of bridge.

Dad loved holidays and celebrations with family and friends, especially Christmas, not just for its religious significance but for its element of laughter and fun. Dad was Santa Claus, and Dad was all of Santa's helpers too! He loved to give gifts and spent weeks before Christmas painting and straightening trkes and bikes, adding to the model train collection or creating some magical masterpiece to put under the Christmas tree.

The greatest material gift Dad cherished in his life besides his home and garden was Pinewood, the cozy little hideaway on Anderson Island built by the combined talents of his family. The fact that there was a golf course on the island made it perfect! Dad loved Pinewood, the trees, the water and wildlife, the clear air. It was a special place to share with family and friends and embodied for him all of the beauty of the Northwest.

And now, Dad... A Time for Tears and a Time to Die...

For all of his days on earth, Dad had a plan for each. He set his goals and found the delicate balance of time for every purpose under heaven. His last hours on earth culminated all of the things he loved. He celebrated Ascension Thursday liturgy here with Mom. He spent some time at Pinewood with his close friend, Bud, cleaning out the weeds and paying his annual golf fees. There were friends over the night before to play cards. He bought bedding plants for his garden and a Mother's Day gift for Mom. And then very simply, at home, in Mom's arms, this gentle man slipped away to his new life with God.

He did all of this just as he would have planned. He did not suffer. He did not lose his ability to work or use his hands. He had done everything in life he wanted to. He had fought the fight and won the race. He spoke freely of his departure and how he looked forward to a reunion of all friends and even meeting his own Dad whom he never knew. He wanted his life and death to be a Celebration!

Like the ripples of a Kansas wheat field, the ripples of this simple farm boy's life are that he did achieve greatness, he did achieve wealth. He was a true Patriarch, a teacher of life; a man listened to and respected... a man truly loved.

Johnny's 12 children carried their father to his final resting place.

The birds circled twice and flew upward into the clouds.

The procession to Holyrood Cemetery under cloudy skies was long and memorable. As the people gathered at the grave site, Vince and Larry each deposited cages of their homing pigeons on the green lawn just out of sight. After the prayers, granddaughters Jennifer and Tara with flute and clarinet played "On Eagle's Wings." Suddenly there was a fluttering of wings as the cages opened and some 30 birds circled several times, and then soared upward till they disappeared into the clouds. Abruptly, it turned windy and a drenching shower sent us back to our cars.

The ladies of the parish had a beautiful buffet awaiting us at home on our return from the cemetery. People were served indoors and outdoors under suddenly sunny skies.

Later, Johnny's clothes were returned to me. In the pocket of his favorite Pendleton was scribbled "The Sportsman's Prayer."

I pray that I may live to fish until my dying day

And when it comes to my last cast, I then most humbly pray

When in the Lords great landing net, and peacefully asleep

That in His mercy, I be judged big enough to keep!

Farewell, my love. I knew you were a keeper.

Consolation

For months after Johnny's death I thought about his new life. Having always had a great love and strong belief in the communion of saints I didn't hesitate to have a lot of one-sided conversations with him. I wanted to be reassured that he truly was in heaven. I asked him to send me a sign, and a specific sign at that. I asked him to send a rose, and I didn't want to see just any rose, I wanted a fresh rose given personally to me by someone special. That very evening, Rose Mary stopped by to introduce me to a friend. We chatted for a bit, they left, and I headed to the kitchen to fix my dinner. Then the doorbell rang. It was Rose.

"I almost forgot to give you this."

Wrapped in clear plastic was a miniature rose in full bloom, plus a tiny bud. She continued to explain that her assistant had given it to her with great pride because she had grown it from a cutting. Rose Mary knew I loved roses so she wanted to give it to me. Then she left.

This rose was so beautiful, only the size of my thumbnail. I went to look for my "dandelion vase," the glass toothpick container that served to hold the dandelions and small flowers my sweet children would pick for their mommy. As I admired it I marveled how only God could create such a lovely flower and with that thought came the memory of my request for a sign.

Here it was, carried out in detail! A fresh rose, put in my hand personally, "special" because it had been grown from a cutting, and "special" because the person who gave it to me was our daughter, *Rose.*

As for Johnny's sending me a sign—

How wonderful! What more can I say?

My husband, C. John Schuler 1906 - 1986.

CHAPTER ELEVEN

ON EAGLE'S WINGS AND OTHER FLIGHTS

Dark Night

The story I am about to share could be named "the anatomy of a nervous breakdown." Ultimately, it became a spiritual experience that deepened my faith, saved my life, and delivered me from a five day journey through an earthly "hell." It was many years in the making having its roots in my childhood memories.

Through no fault of their own my parents had suffered severe losses—including their farm—which began our descent into poverty. Life was a struggle, a constant worry about meeting the bare necessities. My father had several serious illnesses as the family grew in size and number. It didn't help that Kansas became a dust bowl following a severe drought, curtailing our ability to produce our own food. Then during my teenage years the Great Depression changed the course of my life. I was unable to continue High School at Mount St. Scholastica Academy due to both parents' ill health. I was told that I was needed at home. As the economy worsened, instead of pursuing my education, I became a "hired girl," working endless hours cooking, cleaning and caring for an elderly stroke victim among other jobs. It is hard to believe I was paid a mere $15 a month. Some months that figured out to less than 50 cents a day.

All of this background is to explain why I had such a drive to accumulate a fund. Of course, that couldn't happen while my husband and I were raising our family. Insurance agents were aghast to know that we had no life insurance on our "bread-winner." That was impossible because Johnny's high blood pressure made him ineligible. We were able to meet our needs with faith, Divine Providence and good management of every dollar. But save? Not a chance! When our youngest child was three I began a day care service, which I continued for 13 years. Since we had managed all through the years without that income I was determined to save it, and save it I did.

Eventually, my savings and the proceeds from the sale of our lower lot—that deep back yard that served as garden, play-ground, party venue and picnic spot for so many years—were invested in a small portfolio and a mutual fund. They were doing just fine, but our broker called repeatedly to convince us that he could really do well for us with "puts and calls." This was foreign to us; I couldn't understand it and would hand the phone to Johnny. At last, he gave consent. Our very next statement showed that we had gained several thousand dollars. We were both very pleased and celebrated by getting our spring supply of bedding plants. At noon that very day, May 9, 1986, at age 79 Johnny's "call" came suddenly. He collapsed and died at home, the place he loved and constantly tried to improve for his family.

Now, as a widow, there needed to be some legal changes. Did I want to continue? Up to this time I hadn't learned a thing. So yes, why not? Six months later my account had grown by one third. I had never told my family and had great hopes of surprising them with a substantial gift once I reached my goal for my retirement fund.

Then, the bad news. . . Around January 17, 1987, eight months after Johnny's death I had a call from the broker warning me that "we are in a little trouble with your account and are selling what we must to cover 'the calls.'" The next mail brought some very scary figures and I began to panic. Because

I had not shared any of this with my family I had no one with whom to discuss my distress. As the hours and days wore on I became so panicked, so stressed I couldn't eat or sleep. I just prayed night and day. I knew by the confirmation slips that it was not over.

Monday would have been our 50th wedding anniversary. The family had gathered Sunday evening to show me their love and caring. I managed to get through the evening without sharing the terror that I was experiencing—a terrible fear that I would lose my home. I had just learned that it had been listed as collateral in the investment agreement. What I feared most—my worst case scenario—was having to tell my children that I had lost my home, the home they grew up in and all loved so much.

So the agony went on a few more days and the confirmation slips in the mail told me that we had lost everything we'd gained plus more. Small comfort, but I was thankful I was alone in the house so no one would know how distraught I was. My digestive system had shut down completely. I really wondered if I would die. I was so shattered I couldn't sleep. I just prayed night and day to every saint in Heaven to intercede for me. I remember praying to the Poor Souls that I could sleep. Eventually, I did fall asleep.

It was then that I experienced in a dream the comfort only our loving God can give. In my dream, I was standing alone by a lovely river in a beautiful mountain setting. I could hear its song as the clear water flowed over the rocks and pebbles. The sky was very blue. I recall feeling the beauty and serenity of the scene when I saw something, a black spot in the sky. It grew closer and soon I realized it was a large bird flying toward me. It swooped down and landed at my feet. I bent over to touch it when it hopped up into my hands. Then it spread its big wings and completely embraced me, calmly staying there while snuggling its head under my chin. Suddenly I realized that this bird was an eagle. And with that the words of Psalm 91 set to music came to me, "I will bear you up on eagles' wings," and I felt so peaceful. Soon, I awoke. The weight was lifted. I felt no more panic. I was at peace pondering what I had just experienced in a dream when I realized I was famished! I was so hungry I had to get up and find some food and water.

The peace remained and I became rational and could see the end of this fiasco. I had less than we started with, but after all, there is only one of us now and it didn't seem important. I thank God I had survived this terrible ordeal. My shattered dreams of surprising the family were modified to say the least. I knew that I would never again put so much importance on the accumulation of money, at least not by taking risks. The following year was the stock market crash of '87, which again reduced the savings we had worked so hard to gain. But I had learned to "let go and let God."

Finding Myself

After the shock of Johnny's sudden death, accepting this new phase of my life took some soul searching. I recall attending a parish meeting. We were asked to introduce ourselves with a short statement. When it came my turn, in truth and almost in tears, I said: "I'm Dorothy Schuler and right now I'm not sure who I am."

I trusted in God's promise to "bear me up on eagle's wings" but after sharing decisions for almost fifty years with the "head of the family," it took some time to trust myself to make decisions alone. I definitely wanted to be strong and independent but it didn't come automatically. With small steps and with the love and approval of family I began to feel more confident and life's journey became smoother.

The Graduate

One of the first things I did was to enroll in North Seattle Community College to get my General Education Diploma. I had heard of a fellow parishioner who had done it. She was from the Midwest with a history similar to mine. Since I had never heard of "GED" I was excited and inspired about erasing a pernicious stigma from my past.

Over the years I had carried that deep, dark secret. I didn't want anyone to know that I had to drop out after one year of high school. I put myself on the bottom rung of the ladder and thought I was stuck there. I was sure I was inferior to everyone. My next door neighbor constantly reminded me of her college days and was curious about my schooling. I didn't lie but gave subtle references to school at Mount St. Scholastica and said I was in the class of '34—which was true!

When my kids were in grade school and it was suggested to me that I run for president of the Mothers Club, I immediately and emphatically declined. "I'd never have the time to be a good president." That was true even if I'd had a Ph.D, but I couldn't risk revealing my secret.

At my "graduation" with my daughters, Carol and Rose, 1986.

At age seventy I received my General Education Diploma. I was touched that my family was so proud of me. In their typical fashion they all gathered to give me a private graduation ceremony, complete with "Pomp and Circumstance" music. Of course, as conceived by them, I received additional honors. They presented a "scholarship" to the University of Washington and a big medal on a ribbon honoring me as valedictorian in my age group (of course, I was the only one). It was a spirit-lifting event. Even if I couldn't take credit for my own graduation at the proper age, I had proudly celebrated the many graduations of my sons and daughters and grandchildren from high school and university.

A dear friend declared "Dorothy Schuler, there is a vast difference between wisdom and knowledge. Now we know you have both."

The House Mother

Little did I know that over the next dozen years my empty nest would be filled to capacity with university students, future doctors, lawyers, dentists, a rocket scientist, a ballerina, visiting faculty and students from Japan, China, Africa, Italy,

Columbia, and France. They were of different religions and cultures. What a wonderful and dynamic mix of people, the first of which was one of my day care children who remembered the upstairs bedrooms and knew they were empty. I still recall her saying, "Mrs. Schuler can I come live with you?" More than one was turned away because we had a full house. I enjoyed those years.

Once again I was able to add to my retirement fund but with a different attitude. I wasn't so driven and I could give myself permission to enjoy my life. I had several trips to Europe, and a whole month in Africa. I visited Rome, Germany, London and Prague. I also bought a new car which I drove for almost twenty five years. Recently, I traded it in for a newer model. I've had my house repaired, re-roofed, painted, carpeted and redecorated. I've replaced windows, gutters and fence, and generally maintained our beloved home, which is now over 100 years old. We are growing old together. I thank a loving, Providential God for all the years when He "bore me up on eagles wings." It has been my joy and pleasure to tithe to the parish to try to give back to the Lord what He so caringly provided for me.

The Model

Along with the fun of having young folks in my home, one of my renters led me by pure serendipity to a short career in TV commercial modeling. The young woman from New York needed a ride to a modeling agency where she had an appointment. While she was being interviewed another lady sat beside me and began a conversation. She asked if I would be interested in becoming a model for commercials. I assured her that I would not as I had no experience whatever. She reassured me that they often get calls for "seniors" for medical ads. I learned then that she was the owner of the agency. The next day a talent scout came to my home to encourage me and I agreed to take an acting course in preparation. After the course I began to get calls for auditions. I never got a big break like Clara Peller, the Wendy's "Where's the Beef" lady, who

In a commercial for the Bon Marche.

launched her TV modeling career at age 82 and made a lot of money doing it, but over a period of five years I was chosen to film a number of commercials. I did a corporate video for Microsoft, a couple of catalog shoots for the Bon Marche (now Macy's), a commercial for Taco del Mar, an infomercial for Rug Doctor and another for a health drink. At that point I was heading for a heart attack and felt too tired to audition. The gig was fun while it lasted and I met a lot of lovely people. Wouldn't have missed it for the world!

The Traveler

From the time I was a child, nothing ever stopped my desire to find out what lay beyond my little world.

My international travel started in 1975 when Johnny and I made a thrilling trip to Rome. Before he died we had just one more trip together, this time a 1983 vacation to Mexico with friends. These excursions gave me a taste of travel and a desire to see more of the world. After Johnny's death I had several memorable trips to Europe, numerous journeys within the USA and one to Africa. The little girl who wanted to see beyond the view had the privilege of exploring three continents, seeing the glorious capitals of Europe, the bush of Africa

On a winter trip to the beach with my daughter, Joan.

and the splendor of our own fifty States, including Alaska and Hawaii. In the process I gained a glimpse into other cultures and worlds I didn't even know existed—from the slums of Nairobi to the grandeur of Rome—and I was enriched by the amazing people I met along the way.

One of my most memorable trips was my 1990 "expedition" to Africa, thanks to the encouragement and generosity of my daughter, Marge, definitely a world traveler. She was sure I'd love it. So together with Marge and my sister Lucy, I experienced Africa.

From a close up and personal look into a poor rural village of Maasai in Kenya, to dining in elegance in Harare, Zimbabwe, we explored Africa for a full month. We enjoyed the dancing, singing and music of the various tribes at hotels, lodges and authentic villages. We had a look into the history and culture of another continent, and for me geography came alive. We saw cultural and economic differences. Some people wore traditional garb, some gray flannel suits. Some were fully urbanized, others still at home only in the rural villages. Some, probably the majority, were somewhere symbolically between the village and the city struggling for a good life.

In Nairobi, Kenya and Harare, Zimbabwe (at that time a lovely city), we enjoyed charming hotels, beautifully prepared food, swimming pools, parks, art galleries, sculpture gardens, abundant taxis and other services. An especially thrilling experience for me was attending Mass at the Cathedral of the Sacred Heart in Harare filled to overflowing. Led by a choir and drums, the entire congregation sang in harmony; it was the most beautiful sound I have ever heard. Even the smallest children sang their praises to God with dancing.

I loved the trip to Amboseli Game Park in southeastern Kenya with the spectacular backdrop of Mount Kilimanjaro. We drove many miles over rough and dusty roads in our Nissan van, our first experience of safari. A sudden greening of the landscape with acacia trees and other growth brought forth a myriad of exotic animals. We were convinced we were in Africa when a pair of elephants trumpeted their annoyance, and when Maasai tribesmen with spears protested our taking pictures of their cattle.

The most spectacular scene, of course, was one of the wonders of God's creation, Victoria Falls, one and one half miles across and double the height of Niagara. Under a cloudless blue sky

In a Maasai village, Kenya.

we cruised on the Zambezi River above the falls where we saw crocodiles and hippos. The hotel at "Vic Falls" was elegant with winding staircases, formal gardens, a view of the lush greens surrounding the river with the ascending spray of the falls. We breakfasted on the veranda. A couple of monkeys dropped out of the trees, took some of our food and in a flash were back in the treetop eating and chattering—probably saying about us, "Don't they look silly in those clothes?" On our mile hike to the falls we encountered people selling their wares and a captured python presented to us for dramatic effect. We bought a carved giraffe and could have had everything they had to sell in trade for our Reeboks.

Next, a 35 minute flight to Wange Game Park and another beautiful lodge with a balcony overlooking a watering hole. We were able to see game there all night long. But at noon nearly 40 elephants came out of the bush to enjoy drinks and baths while we sat by the pool and discovered nearly empty cameras. I got one shot.

Back to Harare to have a deeper look into the problems and progress of African women. Marge, after fourteen years with the Maryknoll Sisters had left the community, but continued

Here I am in a typical Sudanese Taub with the Sudanese delegation to the women's conference.

161

her work on social justice issues, particularly women's rights in the third world. That year she organized a conference in Africa on "Women, Law and Development" with participation of women lawyers from all across the continent. We attended several sessions and heard reports from many countries. Each had similar problems affecting women's status, but they also had unique challenges. Some issues, like laws and customs governing inheritance for women and the appalling treatment of widows, were beyond our comprehension. Surely, what seems like a hopeless condition of ingrained attitudes must eventually change in recognition of the dignity and rights of women. Our prayers are for the victims of injustice and for those who work for justice.

One afternoon, Lucy and I decided to skip the conference to take a walk and enjoy the beautiful weather. We were just a few blocks on our way when we came upon a lovely park. There were many hawkers selling carvings, necklaces, bracelets and dangling ear beads. We would have bought some items if there had only been a few vendors, but not with fifteen or twenty all in our face competing for a sale. So we did as we were advised, "Just say 'no' and keep walking." A few blocks later we were admiring some lovely colonial buildings, one of which read, "The High Court of Zimbabwe."

Lucy said, as she had many times during our trip, "I can't believe I'm here!" "Well," I said, "let me prove it to you in full color. Stand right there and I'll take your picture." I was just snapping the shot when a long, slim, black hand was on my camera. I reacted immediately with an emphatic, "No, you can't have my camera!" By this time, Lucy was at my side. "Dorothy," she whispered in her best ventriloquist imitation, "I think he is a policeman." I noticed the long barreled pistol hanging from his holster as he issued a command. "Come with me."

We crossed the street, approached one of the colonial buildings we had been admiring and entered a crowded room with other people—waiting to be booked, I assumed. After a

Lucy looking at the Harare High Court.

conversation with a grim-looking magistrate, the policeman demanded my camera. I explained he could have the film but not the camera. He did not respond, rather he summoned a large uniformed matron and motioned for us to follow her. She led us down a long red-carpeted corridor. She guided us into a small room.

"Wait here!" she demanded and left us to wonder what next. Knowing I had "adopted" St Raphael to take care of us on our trip, Lucy quipped, "Where is your St Raphael when we need him?"

Just then a handsome young man came in to speak to us and quietly said "Did you know it is against the law to take pictures of a government building?"

"Of course not. No one told us that."

He left the room and moments later the powerful matron lady came back to return us to the magistrate. Suddenly they handed me my camera—with the film still there. We were free to go and they never even asked our names. What a relief! We were so worried that we would embarrass Marge with our misadventure.

Stuck in the mud in Maasai Mara. I took the picture while keeping lookout for hungry lions.

Lucy, Marge and I in Africa.

We returned to our hotel and sheepishly told her about it. She had a good laugh as did the women lawyers attending the conference. Shirin, Member of Parliament and former Attorney General of the island country of Mauritius, assured us that she and the others would have defended us. Fortunately that wasn't needed. I thanked St Raphael. I think he took care of the matter very well.

After Harare we went back to the excitement of Safari. When the conference ended we returned to Nairobi, this time to go to Maasai Mara, a huge savannah that supports thousands of wild animals, which we hunted with cameras. We crossed the Great Rift Valley over washed out roads to reach our lodge where we slept in tents. Our early morning and late evening game drives yielded our first sight of lions feasting on a buffalo with other animals lined up waiting their turn. We saw elephants, giraffes, impalas, gazelles, kudus, cape buffalo, baboons, zebras, lions, cheetah, wildebeests, storks, buzzards, and more. It was a memorable, fantastic experience.

Had a wonderful time, wish you'd been there!

The Computer

Earlier, my writing experience was limited to hand written letters to family and friends. When I started to write my memoir I received a lot of moral encouragement from my kids along with suggestions and material aids to make the process easier, including stacks of yellow pads and pens, books on memoir writing, even a beautiful paperweight engraved with a suggested title of my book. But the most challenging aid I received was a computer! "Oh," they told me, "it is easy and you'll be able to edit right there and not have to rewrite over and over." It sounded good, but I wasn't entirely convinced.

So it was with excitement and more than a little fear and trepidation that I began to do battle with that incredible invention on my desktop. I, who never learned to type properly—relying instead on a minimal effort in hunt and peck—dared to think I could learn to control this ingenious product of modern technology. As I struggled with what seemed an impossible accomplishment to learn to type, outfoxing that irascible mouse that can make hours of work vanish at the slightest false or accidental touch became the first order of business. Only then could I begin the task of gathering my memories and recording them with the hope that the words and tunes would flow in a readable account.

The computer enthusiasts among my kids were confident that I could master it. They also thought that I was indestructible and would live to the age of 140. I only hoped that it would not take that long to hear them quote Professor Henry Higgins, telling Eliza in My Fair Lady, "You've got it, you've got it! By George, I think you've got it." Well, a dozen years have passed since then.

In the end, let's just say I prefer to write longhand. I did, however, become sufficiently fluent in the computer to use it regularly for email letter writing, paying my bills online, checking the stock market (when I had a portfolio) and logging in to Facebook daily to find out what my friends are up to.

The Grand Salami

I was feeling prosperous one Christmas and wanted to do something that would be a knockout! I asked for suggestions and Jim and Bev came up with a winner. It was when our Seattle Mariners baseball team was extremely popular and winning their games in the Kingdome. "Reserve a section for the entire family and lots of friends." And what a gift it was, with a most exciting game with triple plays and home runs with bases loaded and Dave Neihaus announcing: "get out the rye bread Grandma, here comes a grand salami." And it happened! An unforgettable party.

Celebration

For my eightieth birthday my family organized a beautiful reception, buffet and program in the St. Benedict's School school auditorium. A highlight was the presentation of a pair of ruby slippers and the revelation that I am really "Dorothy from Kansas" who came to the "Emerald City," Seattle, of course. My family and my friends from the parish and far beyond filled the crowded auditorium. I have memories of a beautiful Sunday Mass where my twelve children, one by one, brought me a rose. By the time I held a bouquet of a dozen red roses, everyone was in tears, including the birthday girl.

For my ninetieth birthday, they outdid themselves once again. What a grand celebration!

It began with a concelebrated Mass, carefully planned by our pastor, Father Steve Sallis, and the four concelebrating priests. The music, the readings, the flowers and every detail were selected with exquisite attention. I hope I will never forget any small part of that memorable hour. Then all the guests gathered in the school auditorium, transformed by the genius of my talented family into an elegant reception room with tables beautifully set to serve the guests. Two hundred and thirty friends, from as far away as Kansas, Texas, Oregon, and California all honored me with their presence. My four living siblings, Leo, Dick, Lucy and John (Bud) and some of their children—my nieces and nephews—were among the guests.

A highlight of the program following the luncheon was a family-produced DVD video that drew on old snapshots, formal portraits, "Super 8" movies, and video recordings to tell my life history. Afterwards, ninety members of my family, each holding a candle (yes, ninety candles) led the singing of "Happy Birthday." Then came the total surprise: Sister Philomine of the Benedictine Sisters from Atchison, Kansas presented me with an authentic Mount St. Scholastica's high school diploma. It took seventy-one years and a lifetime of

Sons, daughters, spouses, grandchildren and great grandchildren gather at my eightieth birthday celebration.

Mass at St. Benedict's church, celebrated by our pastor, Fr. Steve Sallis, with con-celebrants Frs. Jack Walmsley, Tim Clark, James Picton and Michael McDermott. Grandson Jacob was the server. This was for my ninetieth birthday.

learning experience to achieve it, but no one will ever know how touching it was for me to receive that honor.

Every member of the family contributed effort, talent and love to give their mother a grand celebration. It must have succeeded because the beauty of the moment inspired all those present to stand in ovation. Is it possible to be humble and proud at the same time? Words can never express what I felt that wonderful day!

"Dorothy from Kansas" receiving a toast at my
eightieth birthday party, wearing my ruby slippers!

POST SCRIPT

The few stories I tell in this book are only a small sample of the happenings along the path of my life journey, and despite the ups and downs of living, it has been a wonderful ride. Because God has always shown me the way, I feel gratitude that at age ninety-five can still say "I will go, Lord, if you lead me."

Yes, I've made the decisions and the choices that got me to this point, but God's guidance has always been there. As a child, I wanted to see "beyond the bend," and when I grew up I found Johnny who helped me follow that dream. In following the path of motherhood I have been rewarded beyond imagining.

My "promised land" turned out to be my family, my parish church and community, and the wonderful friends who have graced my life over the past many years here in Seattle on Wallingford and, indeed, around the world.

My gratitude is boundless.

Dorothy Schuler
Seattle, Washington
February, 22, 2011

Dorothy's Prayer

The Lord is my shepherd. I shall not want.

In verdant pastures he gives me repose in the scenic beauty of the magnificent Northwest.

By the still waters of Green Lake He leads me,
He refreshes my soul.

My parish church is my refuge,
He sets the table before me,
He anoints my head with oil in the sacraments of Grace.

My cup overflows,
Each time I empty my hands
He fills them up.

I fear no evil,
He gives me courage.

Goodness and Kindness will follow me
the remaining days of my life.

May I dwell in the house of the Lord, the heavenly promised land,
To praise Him and thank him forever and ever.

Amen

Adapted from Psalm 23

Appendix 1: MY CHILDREN

A Schuler Family Update

This year, 2011, my youngest child is in his 50th year, my oldest in his 74th, and I'm in my 96th. I think it is safe to say we have beaten the odds!

Most of my children have become grandparents themselves and they all have unique and caring stories to tell about their own lives. When we gather for family events, it is my happiness to see *all* my sons and daughters down the generations. My joy is tempered only by some sadness that my hearing loss denies me the pleasure of conversations with the little children. Yet, how fortunate I have been to see them grow and develop over many decades.

I dreamed as a young bride seventy five years ago of raising a family rooted in the values of our faith, in service to others and love of family. I can say that I am immensely proud of them for their place in the world. Whether plumber or Ph.D., homemaker or humanitarian, they have all helped create a more livable, beautiful and just world.

And once again, I sing my Deo Gratias!

We had eight children in 1950, two years after we moved to Wallingford.

There were ten in 1957. This is a picture taken on the occasion of a visit to Seattle by my brother Paul (back row, second left.)

This photo was taken at Paul's baptism in December of 1961. The
ceremony was officiated by Archbishop Thomas J. Connolly.

This was the first family picture taken with all twelve children. It was
1964.

Here we are at Vince's wedding. Again, all but Marge are present. The year was 1965.

Here is the family all grown up, around 1983.
Front from left: Rose Mary, Joan, Johnny, myself, Marge and Carol.
Back: David, Vince, Larry, Jack, Jim, Greg, Joe and Paul.

Here I am with my twelve children at my 80th birthday celebration. They are standing in order of birth. counterclockwise. Next to me is Jack, then Marge, Jim, Vince, Carol, Larry, Rose Mary, David, Joan, Greg, Joe and Paul. This was in 1995.

Below is the last photo taken of me with all twelve in 2001.

Recent pictures of my children. It is rare to get everyone together at the same time. Only Jack is missing in the picture of my "boys," taken in 2010.

Appendix 2: My Siblings

A Meinhardt Family Update

When I was young and my family was going through tough struggles during the decades of the twenties and thirties just to acquire the necessities of life, I always believed that someday we'd "make it." I also knew all my brothers and sisters were precious and I hoped the best for them.

Although three died in childhood or at birth, twelve of us lived to adulthood, eight brothers and three sisters. Four of us survive today.

It is, of course, one of the sorrows of life that we must all suffer the loss of loved ones. Since I've been privileged to live to ninety-five, I've had to say final farewells to most of my family. The inevitable call came for eight of my siblings. They each lived remarkable lives, working with what they were given to become successful, caring human beings. They happily participated in the prosperity of the post-World War II era and all moved beyond the poverty of our childhood to achieve comfort and success in their lives. But it was the faith and work ethic we all acquired from our parents that provided them the best foundation.

I miss them all. I cried when my helpless little brother Archie passed away at age 35, but I knew he was finally relieved of the burden of severe cerebral palsy. I grieved

Above: With my sisters Agnes and Rita, sometime in the 1970s.

Below: John (Bud), Lucy, Leo, Dorothy, Dick, 2005.

at the unexpected and sudden death of my "big" brother, Paul. He had always been an inspiration to me. I felt sorrow for Otto and Oscar, who lived far from me when they arrived at the final days of their lives. I was happy to comfort my affable brother Fred as he approached his death. My heart ached with sorrow as my beautiful little sister, Agnes, struggled through chemotherapy while she stayed with us in Seattle. Her loss at age 55 was a blow. Leo lived to be 92. He died shortly after attending my 90th birthday celebration. Rita, much appreciated by the family, gave unselfishly all her life and died at 85.

Four of us survive. Lucy, 83, lives in Topeka, Dick, 89, near Seattle and John (Bud), 81, in Albuquerque. They are three of the youngest four Meinhardt children. In our older years we stay in touch and keep up with each other's health struggles and family news. I am in constant email or telephone contact with Lucy and I marvel at her spirit of courage, faith and boundless love. Dick, ever the entrepreneur, still manages his business. His optimism and enthusiasm for life is inspiring. Youngest brother Bud, still flying airplanes at age 80, is seriously impressive.

I am proud of my Meinhardt family and the legacy they have all left to current and future generations.

Appendix 3: MY ANCESTORS

The Hunds and the Meinhardts

My father's maternal great grandparents, the Hunds, were the first people in my family to land on American shores. It was 1832, the year Andrew Jackson was elected to his second term as President. Moritz and Maria Magdalena Hund arrived from Baden, Germany with their children, among whom was their eight year-old son, Michael, my great grandfather. They settled in St. Charles, Missouri.

When Michael was 24 he married Mary Gertrude Borgmeyer in June, 1848. Six years later, they, with others of their community decided to relocate to Mankato, Minnesota. They had been told the area offered opportunities for settlers. By then, Michael and Mary Gertrude had three children: Michael, Moritz and Mary Magdelen.

The group left St. Charles by pack train for St. Louis, where they boarded the river steamer, Henrietta, bound for St. Paul, Minnesota. Their cargo consisted of family trunks containing personal belongings, a plentiful supply of food, farm implements, eleven horses, five wagons and a buggy.

The voyage on the steamer went well until they reached Keokuk, Iowa where the heavily laden steamer could go no further because of the shallow water. The women and children remained on board while the men unloaded the cargo, put it on the wagons and went by land fifteen miles to Montrose, Iowa to wait for the Henrietta to arrive. During this two day interlude Mary Gertrude was stricken with cholera. The boat anchored at Montrose and Michael hurried aboard to find his wife near death. When he left her two days before, she was in perfect health. After she died Michael hired a conveyance to take her body thirty-five miles to Burlington, Iowa for burial. Michael's brother John lived six miles from there. While Michael was attending to the funeral of his wife, the Henrietta rammed a rock and suffered severe damage. It would take a month for the ship to resume the voyage. When they finally reached St. Paul, they traveled by land for another week, arriving in Mankato on October 15, 1854, forty-eight days after leaving St. Charles.

Michael immediately began the process of buying a claim. He found and purchased a property that already had a building on the land. It was a beautiful 24' X 16' block house, smooth inside and out because it was made of planed logs. As the community settled in, I presume the families and friends all helped each other to build shelter, maybe log cabins and barns.

Next order of business: Call a meeting to make plans for a parish. On the Sunday between Christmas and New Years in 1854 fourteen Catholic men answered the call. Michael Hund was a leader among this group. He lent the first $200.00 to purchase the land. He also donated the block house on his property to be used as a temporary church until a permanent one could be built. Services were held there for the 18 families that made up the new Catholic parish of Sts. Peter and Paul. When he was legally able to move the house to the land purchased for the church, the men dismantled it, hauled it by oxen team the one mile from Agency Hill to the parish site where the log house was reassembled. Construction on the permanent church began in September 1856 and was completed in 1872. "Hallelujah!" I can hear them saying, "Grosser Gott wir Loben Dich." (Holy God we praise Thy Name.) The original block house is still on the site of Sts. Peter and Paul parish in Mankato.

Michael's three children, Mary, Moritz and Michael, were being cared for by their grandparents, the Borgmyers, while Michael built a house for his family. Eventually, Michael returned to St. Charles to bring back his parents, Moritz and Maria Magdalena, to his new home in Mankato. While in St Charles Michael met and married his second wife, Otillia Peters. They became the parents of six children, one of whom was my grandma, Frances (1864-1955). The others in the family were: Joseph, Leo, Phillip, Theresa, and Mary. Michael Hund farmed near Mankato for 18 years during a perilous time for settlers in the region. In 1857 a band of Sioux Indians caused panic when they fell upon unsuspecting settlers near Spirit Lake, Iowa murdering 47 people. The Sioux Outbreak of 1862, also known as the Dakota Conflict, began on August 17, 1862, along the Minnesota River in southwest Minnesota. The Hund farm was only a few miles from New Ulm when it came under attack by the Sioux in August of 1862. At this time the country was engaged in the Civil War and few troops

My great grandfather, Michael Hund
1824-1898

were available to control the conflict, but a volunteer group came from Mankato to save the town from the Indian uprising. For the next ten years farming in that region of Minnesota continued to be a challenge as skirmishes continued and most of the immigrants fled.

Sometime around 1872 Michael heard about a new possibility for a better life in America. A Jesuit priest from St. Marys, Kansas had spread the word to immigrants that a German Catholic community had been formed in Newbury Township in mid-eastern Kansas. Land allocated by the US. Government to the Pottawatomie Indians as a reservation became available when the Indians began selling parcels to settlers.

Michael's elderly parents had probably died by then and in the spring of 1873 Michael and Otillia lost their 12 year old daughter, Mary. This must have been the deciding factor because the following year the Hund family packed all their belongings into their covered wagons and set out for Kansas. Grandma (Francis Hund) was ten at the time and loved to ride horses. She told us she rode most of the trip side saddle as girls were expected to do. She also took pride in letting us know she could beat anyone at a race, even her brothers. I wish I could have heard more of this trip overland in covered wagons.

Otillia (Peters) Hund 1828-1921. I remember when my great grandmother Hund died. I was six years old. Here she is with one of her daughters, possibly my grandma, Frances (Hund) Meinhardt.

Once in Kansas, Michael Hund acquired 420 acres of land, one and a half miles southwest of Newbury. There he established a wheat farm with a section allocated for an orchard of peach and apple trees. Motivated by his success in Kansas, many of the Hund family friends in Minnesota followed him to Newbury. Michael, who had been a leader of the Mankato community, continued to play that role in his new township. He was elected Justice of the Peace and town trustee several times and was one of nine families who built the first Catholic church in Newbury in 1874. It was a frame building costing $614.84.

Michael died in 1898. His obituary states that he had a large and impressive funeral. About 75 carriages took part in the procession to Sacred Heart Cemetery.

It was three years after they arrived in Kansas that Michael's daughter, Frances, met my grandfather, August Meinhardt (1853–1915). Frances was fifteen at the time, August was 27. My brother Leo relates a story Grandma told him about this. She had two "gentlemen callers," August Meinhardt and another young man also an immigrant farmer named Meinhardt, but not related to August. It seems the other young

My grandfather, August Meinhardt
1853-1915

man was shy, so August made a proposal: each gentleman would go to a different corner of the parlor, and Francis would choose the one to spend the evening (and ultimately, the rest of her life) with, and the other would leave. Of course, she walked toward the one who had proposed the solution. She was sixteen when she married August in 1880.

August was a German immigrant from Silberhausen in the Eichfeld region of Saxony in Germany. He was the son of Johannes Nikolaus Meinhardt and Elizabeth Brand. When he was about 17 years old, August deserted from the Prussian Army and came to America. In order to leave Germany he had to stow away on a ship, since by that time, German authorities required emigrants to seek release from German citizenship before leaving. This policy allowed them to identify those who might be leaving with unfulfilled military or other obligations. It seems that as late as 1900, the authorities were still trying to find August, who was by then 47 years old, the patriarch of a large family and a successful farmer in Kansas.

The ship on which August stowed away took him to England. He must have had some savings or he worked in England to gain the funds needed for passage because in 1871 he set sail from Liverpool. His original intent was to go to Argentina, but when he reached New York, his ship's first port of call, he decided to stay in the United States.

Perhaps my grandfather heard the famously quoted words of Horace Greeley, "Go West. Go West young man and grow up with the country," because August decided to do just that. He got as far as Davenport, Iowa where he taught school for a time. From there he went to St. Louis to study English and worked in a tannery. At some point he was dispatched to Kansas on business related to the acquisition of hides and learned that land was becoming available there. This was the break he was waiting for. He promptly moved to Kansas in pursuit of his American Dream.

In 1883 at age 30, three years after he and Frances married, August acquired 450 acres of bottom land near Paxico, which

August and Frances (Hund) Meinhardt with their seven children. My father, John Leo, is the oldest. This picture was taken in 1897 when he was about 16.

he purchased directly from a Pottawatomie Indian, Wah-Ka-Zo, for the sum of $250. August became a well known, well-respected cattle feeder. August Meinhardt and Frances Hund had seven children. Their first child was my father, John Leo Meinhardt.

My father, John Leo
Meinhardt 1881-1939

My Father's Ancestral Chart

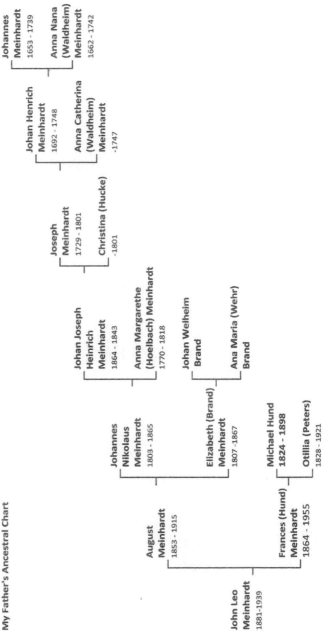

Johannes Meinhardt
1653 - 1739

Anna Nana (Waldheim) Meinhardt
1662 - 1742

Johan Henrich Meinhardt
1692 - 1748

Anna Catherina (Waldheim) Meinhardt
-1747

Joseph Meinhardt
1729 - 1801

Christina (Hucke)
-1801

Johan Joseph Heinrich Meinhardt
1864 - 1843

Anna Margarethe (Hoelbach) Meinhardt
1770 - 1818

Johan Welheim Brand

Ana Maria (Wehr) Brand

Johannes Nikolaus Meinhardt
1803 - 1865

Elizabeth (Brand) Meinhardt
1807 -1867

Michael Hund
1824 - 1898

Otillia (Peters)
1828 - 1921

August Meinhardt
1853 - 1915

Frances (Hund) Meinhardt
1864 - 1955

John Leo Meinhardt
1881-1939

The Tillmanns

My mother's parents, Joseph Tillmann, and Anna Schmitz Kolde, came from Rheinland, Germany (Prussia).

Joseph Heinrich Tillmann (1850-1928) was the first child of Henry Joseph Tillmann and Walburga Edelman of Schiefsbahn, Germany. As a young farmer, he was disappointed when the young woman he hoped to marry, Anna Schmitz (1852-1916), married Bernard Kolde, an artist from Bersenbruck, Lower Saxony. Five years later, Bernard died and Anna moved with her children to Osterath to be with her parents. It was then that Joseph proposed marriage to Anna and she accepted. Joseph and Anna were married on October 28, 1883. Anna's two children, Peter and Gertrude, attended the wedding. After their marriage Joseph and Anna had 6 children, 3 girls and 3 boys. One of the girls was my mother, Dena.

Motivated by the desire to avoid compulsory military service for their sons, Joseph and Anna left Germany in December, 1892 and boarded the SS Belgenland at Antwerp, Belgium. My mother told me that her father had sewn his fortune, $4000 in cash, into the lining of his suit for the trip. She also entertained us with stories about stormy weather and scary moments on the voyage and her excitement when the family finally arrived at Ellis Island, New York on January 13, 1893.

From there, they made their way to Kansas with hopes for a bright future, but like many immigrant families of the time, they faced new challenges and sometimes wrenching losses. Within three weeks of arrival in Paxico, Joseph and Anna lost all three sons and one daughter from the measles or some other infectious disease contracted during the trip. Only their two oldest daughters, Burgie and Dena, were spared.

My mother remembered coming home from the funeral of the third little brother only to get the sad news of the death of the baby sister. Their names were Andrew, Henry, William and Marie.

"A German family by the name of Tillmann, living on the Blane farm northeast of Newbury, have had a sad experience since coming to Wabaunsee County but a few days more than a month ago. On Sunday last, they buried one of their children in the Newbury cemetery--the fourth within ten days. When they arrived at New York the health officers came aboard and for more than two hours the steerage passengers were drawn up in line on deck--in the cold wind--to be vaccinated. They contracted severe colds by the unnecessary exposure and with vaccine virus clogged up in their systems they contracted the measles. It is a sad experience but with the facts before us, the great wonder is that a single member survives" Alma Signal Newspaper, February 25, 1893

So Grandpa and Grandma were left with their two daughters, Burgie and Dena, and Anna's two children, Peter and Gertrude. Later, two other girls were born to the family, Dorothy and Christine. Pete and Gertie were soon off to find work in Topeka, leaving Grandpa with no help on his newly purchased farm; no help except for that of the two girls, one of whom was not at all enthused about it! My mother went to school until the fifth grade. After a few years on the farm, she solicited her brother Pete to find work for her in Topeka. So, to the consternation of her parents, when she was about fifteen my mother left home (some say "ran away") to work as a maid in the home of a local millionaire banker's family, the Mulvanes. She never talked about her sojourn in the big city, but it must have been quite an education for her. She married my father in 1906 when she was 21 years old.

Mom's mother died in 1916, shortly after I was born, so I always knew my Grandpa Tillmann as a solitary figure who would come and visit my mother after Mass each day to break his fast and drink his morning cup of coffee. After his wife died Grandpa moved in with my Aunt Burgie, who had been widowed herself by then. I remember how he drove old Daisy and his little buggy to church every day, winter or summer. When there was a blizzard, he walked the three miles. He'd come into church with icicles on his moustache. He didn't speak English, so he didn't have to bother socializing—he just came to pray, and pray and pray.

Joesph and Anna (Schmitz Kolde) Tillmann with their children. My mother, Dena, (top left) was about 14 when this picture was taken.

My mother, Dena Tillmann 1884-1969

My Mother's Ancestral Chart

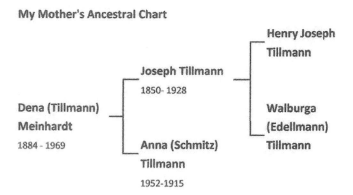

Dena (Tillmann)
Meinhardt
1884 - 1969

Joseph Tillmann
1850- 1928

Anna (Schmitz)
Tillmann
1952-1915

Henry Joseph
Tillmann

Walburga
(Edellmann)
Tillmann

Acknowledgements

I am most grateful to my daughter, Marge, for finding a way to structure a book from bits and pieces written over several years, for her research in verifying times and places mentioned in my story, for editing the manuscript and for guiding me through the process of producing a publishable product.

A special thanks to my children who encouraged me in this endeavor with kind words, books, writing equipment and computer know-how, and who waited patiently through long periods of blank pages for something to emerge. Paul and Nadine provided me with lots of pads and pens. Greg and Stephanie brought me books on memoir writing, as did my friends, Bud and Marian Trebon. Greg donated my first computer. Carol and Joan had lots of ideas about stories I should include. Rose Mary was a cheerleader throughout and kept me going. Jack, Jim, Vince, Larry, David and Joe all joined the chorus with their encouragement.

I thank my sister, Lucy Breitenstein, for her generosity in providing information, photographs and enthusiasm for the project, and my brother, John Meinhardt, for the aerial shots of Newbury and Paxico he took from his plane. I also thank my granddaughter, Tara Tillett, and my daughter-in-law, Stephanie, for typing various parts of the manuscripts from my notes.

Finally, I am grateful to Father Steve Sallis, Louise McDowell, Jean Clancy, Rose Mary Zilmer, Joan Schuler, and Stephanie Schuler, who proofread the manuscript and offered suggestions on how to make it more readable and coherent.

Resources and Credits

Family History

Information on the Meinhardt ancestors comes from the genealogical research of Lucy and Joe Breitenstein conducted in the 1980s at the parish church in Silberhausen in Germany where they examined records of Meinhardt baptisms, weddings, and funerals. The validity of their findings were verified by a German genealogist.

A document about the founding of Sts. Peter and Paul Catholic parish in Mankato, Minnesota from the archives of the church provided information on Michael Hund and his travels to Minnesota. Newspaper articles and data found on Ancestry.com also contributed to the Hund part of the story.

Data on the Tillmann family is from an unpublished monograph prepared in the 1980s by members of the Tillmann Family.

Photographs

Photographs of the Schuler family are from Dorothy Schuler's collection of snapshots covering the period from 1937 to the present with additional photos provided by her children, Greg, Marge, Carol and Joan.

Photographs of the Meinhardt, Hund and Tillmann families are from the collection of Lucy Meinhardt Breitenstein, and cover the period beginning in the 1890s and ending in the 1960s.

Aerial photographs of Newbury and Paxico were taken by John L. Meinhardt.

Cover photo of the author was taken by Greg Schuler.

Comments

In this absorbing and personal tale, you will read about the timeless and true power of family and see that it is not built on wealth or success, but upon relationships, love, service, and sacrifice. If you are tired of books that lecture instead of teach; if you are searching for ways to witness the simple true meaning of life and the power of prayer; if you want to understand the timeless virtues that lead to truly lasting legacies, then Dorothy Schuler's personal journey will bring you home."

Jackie O'Ryan, PBS documentarian, Communications Director at Lakeside School, Seattle, Washington.

Dorothy Schuler was never a victim. She used what is clearly a not insignificant intelligence and gritty ingenuity to face a series of fascinating but daunting challenges. I have a huge admiration for the gutsy determination of this woman who took hold of life with both hands and *lived.*

Terry Herman Sissons, Ph.D., Cambridge England

Dorothy Schuler's delightful and inspiring *My Journey to the Promised Land* is pro-family, pro-faith, pro-life and – on every page through every year – pro-love. Her stories of generations and times now long gone are a treasure and a blessing for all families.

Bill Dodds, Author, Lynnwood, Washington

When my Dad died in August 2003, Dorothy sent me her memoir on her husband Johnny, and the impact of his death. Her words held my attention in a way that surprised me. And I told her afterwards, "You need to write!"

Dorothy Schuler's life is a journey with God and towards God; a journey of faith and utter trust.

Rev. Timothy J. Clark, Our Lady of the Lake Parish, Seattle

12798919R00121

Made in the USA
San Bernardino, CA
28 June 2014